LIVING LITURGY™

FOR EXTRAORDINARY MINISTERS OF HOLY COMMUNION

Year B • 2015

Joyce Ann Zimmerman, C.PP.S.
Kathleen Harmon, S.N.D. de N.
Rev. John W. Tonkin

LITURGICAL PRESS
Collegeville, Minnesota

www.litpress.org

ISSN 1933-3129

ISBN 978-0-8146-3813-2

Presented to

_____

in grateful appreciation
for ministering as an
Extraordinary Minister
of
Holy Communion

_____

_____
(date)

USING THIS RESOURCE

Extraordinary ministers of Holy Communion are called to serve the Christian community by ministering the Body and Blood of Christ to the Body of Christ, for by baptism we are all made members of Christ's Body. Rather than a "status symbol" in the liturgical community, these ministers are servants of the servants, as Jesus himself showed us at the Last Supper. They are called "extraordinary" not because of any personal worthiness or honor, but because the "ordinary" ministers of Holy Communion are bishops, priests, deacons, or instituted acolytes. In the typical parish situation, however, large numbers of the faithful come forward for Communion, and so in most cases lay members of the parish are designated as "extraordinary" ministers so that the Communion procession does not become disproportionately long.

Preparing for this ministry

As with all ministry, extraordinary ministers of Holy Communion must prepare themselves in order to serve their sisters and brothers in Christ well. This book is intended to be a guide and resource for that preparation. Each Sunday and some key festival days are laid out with prayer and reflections to help the Communion minister prepare each week, even when he or she is not scheduled for ministry. Some of the language of the text implies a group is present for the preparation; these texts are conveniently worded for when two or more extraordinary ministers gather for preparation, or for when these texts are shared in the context of the rite of Holy Communion with the homebound and sick.

Holy Communion for the homebound and sick

Jesus' preaching of the Good News in the Gospel is made visible by his many and varied good works on behalf of others. Perhaps more than any other group, Jesus reaches out with his healing touch to those who are sick, and this compassionate ministry continues today in the life of the church. One of the many blessings of parishes who have extraordinary ministers of Holy Communion is that those who are sick or homebound within parishes or those in hospitals and other care centers can share in the liturgical life of the parish more frequently. These ministers are reminded that the sick and suffering share in a special way in Jesus' passion. The ministers can bring hope and consolation and the strength of the Bread of Life to those who seem cut off from active participation in parish life.

Adapting this resource for Holy Communion for the homebound and sick

It is presumed that each Communion minister is familiar with the rites for Communion with the sick. There is a brief rite for those in hospitals or other care centers; this shorter rite is used when the circumstances would not permit the longer rite. The longer rite is used in ordinary circumstances and includes a Liturgy of the Word preceding the Communion rite. When using the longer rite, the opening and closing prayer given for each Sunday or festival included in this book would nicely round out the beginning and end of the service; the gospel is conveniently included to proclaim the word, and a reflection (also included for each Sunday or festival) might be shared.

Privilege and dignity

It is indeed a unique blessing to serve members of the parish as extraordinary ministers of Holy Communion, both at the parish Mass and by bringing Communion to the sick and homebound. The parish's presence through ministry to the sick and homebound is a particular sign of their dignity as members of the Body of Christ. The Communion minister is in a unique position to bring hope and comfort to those who may find little in life to comfort them. May this ministry always be a sign of Jesus' great love and compassion for all his Father's beloved children!

On this First Sunday of Advent we are reminded to be watchful and alert for Christ's Second Coming in future glory. As we begin our prayer and reflection, let us call to mind when we have failed to be watchful and alert . . .

Prayer

Ever-present God who calls us into your divine Presence even now as we await the divine Son's Second Coming, strengthen us to be watchful and alert for the many ways we might serve you, thus hastening the coming of the fullness of your reign. We ask this through Christ our Lord. **Amen.**

Gospel (Mark 13:33-37)

Jesus said to his disciples: "Be watchful! Be alert! You do not know when the time will come. It is like a man traveling abroad. He leaves home and places his servants in charge, each with his own work, and orders the gatekeeper to be on the watch. Watch, therefore; you do not know when the lord of the house is coming, whether in the evening, or at midnight, or at cockcrow, or in the morning. May he not come suddenly and find you sleeping. What I say to you, I say to all: 'Watch!'"

Brief Silence

For Reflection

Four times in this gospel Christ commands us, "Be watchful!" or "Watch!" While we are to watch for Christ's Second Coming, that future can be elusive for us. What is immediate and manageable is to watch for Christ's coming *now* into our midst. Being watchful and alert for the Second Coming is not enough; we must consciously seek to identify Christ already present *now*. If we are proactively watching for everyday encounters with Christ, he will surely not find us "sleeping," neither now nor when he returns. The Second Coming becomes real for us in our encounters with Christ in the here and now. Christ's glory becomes real for us in our encounter with Christ in the here and now. Our watching for Christ's coming is heightened by seeing God in the simple, everyday things we do. We spend Advent in the time and place we always live, and we still can find Christ anew because he is ever making us anew. When we encounter Christ, we actually encounter who we are now and who we are becoming. The work of Advent is to "Be watchful!" so that we grow in being Christ's Presence for others.

✦ The face of each communicant renews my hope in the coming of the Lord by . . .

Brief Silence

Prayer

Bounteous God who feeds us on the Bread of Life and bids us to drink from the Cup of Salvation, help us to grow in our appreciation for the great gift of the Eucharist and to live faithfully its promise of eternal Life. We ask this through Christ our Lord. **Amen.**

In the gospel John the Baptist announces that we must prepare for the One coming who will baptize us with the Holy Spirit. Let us examine during our reflection how well we have lived our baptism this week and allowed the Holy Spirit to change our lives . . .

Prayer

Mighty God, the Spirit you give us is our life and salvation. May we be inspired by the Spirit's indwelling to be humble and gentle, just and self-giving as we, like John the Baptist, live lives that announce the nearness of the risen Christ and the salvation he offers us. We ask this through Christ our Lord. **Amen.**

Gospel (Mark 1:1-8)

The beginning of the Gospel of Jesus Christ the Son of God.

As it is written in Isaiah the prophet: / *Behold, I am sending my messenger ahead of you; / he will prepare your way. / A voice of one crying out in the desert: / "Prepare the way of the Lord, / make straight his paths." /* John the Baptist appeared in the desert proclaiming a baptism of repentance for the forgiveness of sins. People of the whole Judean countryside and all the inhabitants of Jerusalem were going out to him and were being baptized by him in the Jordan River as they acknowledged their sins. John was clothed in camel's hair, with a leather belt around his waist. He fed on locusts and wild honey. And this is what he proclaimed: "One mightier than I is coming after me. I am not worthy to stoop and loosen the thongs of his sandals. I have baptized you with water; he will baptize you with the Holy Spirit."

Brief Silence

For Reflection

John was a desert ascetic whose mission was to prepare the people for a life-transforming change—the Lord is coming! Who is this Lord? One mightier than John. How so? John announces the nearness of salvation; Jesus *is* the salvation. John baptizes with water, Jesus with the Holy Spirit. What does this mean? Jesus' baptism instills God's very Life through the power of the Holy Spirit within us. Baptism with the Holy Spirit transforms our preparation into fulfillment—the Lord has come! Here is the key to grasping John's message: by our encountering the Lord, our own wondering, uncertainty, and searching about the meaning of John's message is dispelled. John's humility as depicted in the words of this gospel ("One mightier than I") did not rest in a false sense of his own worth, but instead on his own deep conviction about who Jesus is, a conviction that only could come from his having encountered the One whom he proclaimed. Like John, we too must personally encounter the very One whose messengers we, too, are to be.

✦ The Lord for me is . . . This Advent I hope to learn that . . .

Brief Silence

Prayer

Your divine Son, O God, comes to us in the wonder of receiving his Body and Blood in Holy Communion. Help us to grow in our own dignity as members of the Body of Christ and act like Jesus taught us in all we do. We ask this through Christ our Lord. **Amen.**

Mary was conceived without sin, remained sinless her whole life, and bore Christ our Lord within her. During our prayer let us ask God to forgive our sins and make us pure and holy . . .

Prayer

God of salvation, who in Mary you give us a model for responding to your divine will with an unreserved yes, be with us as we strive to live lives of grace and holiness that welcome you into our midst. Help us to be ourselves faithful God-bearers as we strive to live as her divine Son taught us. We ask this through Christ our Lord. **Amen.**

Gospel (Luke 1:26-38)

The angel Gabriel was sent from God to a town of Galilee called Nazareth, to a virgin betrothed to a man named Joseph, of the house of David, and the virgin's name was Mary. And coming to her, he said, "Hail, full of grace! The Lord is with you." But she was greatly troubled at what was said and pondered what sort of greeting this might be. Then the angel said to her, "Do not be afraid, Mary, for you have found favor with God. Behold, you will conceive in your womb and bear a son, and you shall name him Jesus. He will be great and will be called Son of the Most High, and the Lord God will give him the throne of David his father, and he will rule over the house of Jacob forever, and of his Kingdom there will be no end." But Mary said to the angel, "How can this be, since I have no relations with a man?" And the angel said to her in reply, "The Holy Spirit will come upon you, and the power of the Most High will overshadow you. Therefore the child to be born will be called holy, the Son of God. And behold, Elizabeth, your relative, has also conceived a son in her old age, and this is the sixth month for her who was called barren; for nothing will be impossible for God." Mary said, "Behold, I am the handmaid of the Lord. May it be done to me according to your word." Then the angel departed from her.

Brief Silence

For Reflection
In Gabriel's address to Mary, the archangel announces what is at the heart of this feast day: "Hail, full of grace! The Lord is with you." Even before assenting to conceiving Jesus by the Holy Spirit, Mary had made "May it be done to me" the abiding habit of her way of relating to God and choosing to do God's will. The relationship between Mary and God had grown all her life to the point where her yes was simply the natural thing for her to do. It didn't take thinking; it was an answer of the heart. When we make choosing to do God's will the abiding habit of our own lives, then like Mary we, too, are filled with God's grace and we, too, bear the Life of the Lord within us.

Rather than shy from God's Presence, Mary welcomed it with her yes. Her emptiness as a virgin is filled by her acceptance of the Lord's coming to her, and a whole new in-breaking of God's Presence happens—of which we receive the inestimable fruits. Surely "nothing [is] impossible for God"!

✦ It is easy for me to say to God "May it be done to me" when . . . It is difficult when . . .

Brief Silence

Prayer
God of love, fill us with your Presence and help us to answer from our very hearts with a yes to whatever you ask of us in our daily living. May we be holy and pure like Mary and one day enjoy everlasting Life with her, offering worship and praise and thanksgiving before your throne of majesty. We ask this through Christ our Lord. **Amen.**

We hear in this gospel how clearly John understood himself to be the voice testifying to Christ, the light. Let us reflect on the times when we have failed to be the voice testifying to Christ, and ask for God's mercy . . .

Prayer

Almighty God, the One who wills that we receive the eternal Life of salvation, guide us in right ways that we might be faithful voices testifying to the Presence of Christ in the everyday circumstances of our lives. We ask this through Christ our Lord. **Amen.**

Gospel (John 1:6-8, 19-28)

A man named John was sent from God. He came for testimony, to testify to the light, so that all might believe through him. He was not the light, but came to testify to the light.

And this is the testimony of John. When the Jews from Jerusalem sent priests and Levites to him to ask him, "Who are you?" he admitted and did not deny it, but admitted, "I am not the Christ." So they asked him, "What are you then? Are you Elijah?" And he said, "I am not." "Are you the Prophet?" He answered, "No." So they said to him, "Who are you, so we can give an answer to those who sent us? What do you have to say for yourself?" He said: / "I am *the voice of one crying out in the desert, / make straight the way of the Lord, /* as Isaiah the prophet said." Some Pharisees were also sent. They asked him, "Why then do you baptize if you are not the Christ or Elijah or the Prophet?" John answered them, "I baptize with water; but there is one among you whom you do not recognize, the one who is coming after me, whose sandal strap I am not worthy to untie." This happened in Bethany across the Jordan, where John was baptizing.

Brief Silence

For Reflection

After saying clearly who he is not ("Christ or Elijah or the Prophet"), John does say who he is: "I am the voice of one crying out in the desert." "Voice": the audible revelation of self. "Crying out": testifying to core convictions. "Desert": place of barrenness and desolation as well as a place of testing and growth. So who is John? The one who in his very being recognizes the Christ who has come to lead the people into the fullness of light and Life. Testifying with conviction to the Light of Christ must be more than speaking words; the conviction is conveyed—cried out—by the way we choose to live each day. Testifying with conviction also means that we must constantly grow in our relationship to Christ and learn to recognize him even where we might not expect to find him. Yes, sometimes we are like the people in the gospel in that we seek the Messiah but often do not recognize his Presence in our midst. The work of Advent is to intensify our good works so that we become attuned to recognizing Christ here and now; even more, it is the work of our whole Christian lives.

✦ Those who come to receive Holy Communion testify for me to the Presence of Christ in that . . .

Brief Silence

Prayer

O God who comes, you call us into the solitude of the desert of our hearts to encounter you and grow into the persons you desire us to become. May we be voices for others who testify to the Gospel values your Son taught, and through our communion with him come to the fullness of Life. We ask this through Christ our Lord. **Amen.**

Long ago God announced to Mary and announces to us now new possibilities for life and salvation. During our prayer and reflection let us call to mind the times when we have not heard God speaking to us nor accepted what God offers us . . .

Prayer

Holy God, you speak to us through the people and events of our lives, faithfully announcing to us your Presence and offering us new Life. May we receive you with open hearts, respond to your will with a trusting yes, and come to know you more fully through the simple acts of goodness we do for others each day. We ask this through Christ our Lord. **Amen.**

Gospel (Luke 1:26-38)

The angel Gabriel was sent from God to a town of Galilee called Nazareth, to a virgin betrothed to a man named Joseph, of the house of David, and the virgin's name was Mary. And coming to her, he said, "Hail, full of grace! The Lord is with you." But she was greatly troubled at what was said and pondered what sort of greeting this might be. Then the angel said to her, "Do not be afraid, Mary, for you have found favor with God.

"Behold, you will conceive in your womb and bear a son, and you shall name him Jesus. He will be great and will be called Son of the Most High, and the Lord God will give him the throne of David his father, and he will rule over the house of Jacob forever, and of his kingdom there will be no end." But Mary said to the angel, "How can this be, since I have no relations with a man?" And the angel said to her in reply, "The Holy Spirit will come upon you, and the power of the Most High will overshadow you. Therefore the child to be born will be called holy, the Son of God. And behold, Elizabeth, your relative, has also conceived a son in her old age, and this is the sixth month for her who was called barren; for nothing will be impossible for God." Mary said, "Behold, I am the handmaid of the Lord. May it be done to me according to your word." Then the angel departed from her.

Brief Silence

For Reflection

God's whole plan of salvation is a perpetual annunciation. In this gospel, there are numerous "annunciations" beyond Gabriel's revealing to Mary that she would conceive "the Son of God." Gabriel makes known that Mary is holy; that the child shall be named Jesus; that the kingdom of this Child would have no end; that this Child is "holy, the Son of God"; that Elizabeth has conceived; that "nothing will be impossible for God"; and that Mary is God's faithful and obedient handmaid. Indeed, perpetual annunciation is God's pattern of relating to us. How do we, then, relate to God? We do so by responding with a yes to God's annunciations in our own lives. God chooses to be known to us, names us holy, and desires that we be filled with God's Life. God's annunciations of saving Presence can come to us in so many ways. Yes, God speaks to us during times of prayer. But God also speaks to us through the everyday persons and events of our lives. Yes is not simply a word. Deepening our relationship with God and others happens when our yes becomes a way of living.

✦ Like Mary, I am a Christ-bearer most effectively when I say yes to God in these ways . . .

Brief Silence

Prayer

In the gift of Holy Communion, O God, you offer us the nourishment we need to make our yes to your divine will a daily way of living. May the annunciations of your Presence to us grant us strength and conviction. We ask this through Christ our Lord. **Amen.**

The great mystery of salvation we celebrate is that God's only-begotten Son became flesh and dwells among us. We pause during our prayer to ponder this great mystery and reflect on whether we have been open to the salvation God offers . . .

Prayer

God of salvation, during this glorious festival of the birth of your divine Son we celebrate a new in-breaking of your divine Presence. Help us to receive your many gifts to us and through them make known your Son's saving Presence among us today. We ask this through Christ our Lord. **Amen.**

Gospel (Luke 2:1-14; from the Mass at Midnight)

In those days a decree went out from Caesar Augustus that the whole world should be enrolled. This was the first enrollment, when Quirinius was governor of Syria. So all went to be enrolled, each to his own town. And Joseph too went up from Galilee from the town of Nazareth to Judea, to the city of David that is called Bethlehem, because he was of the house and family of David, to be enrolled with Mary, his betrothed, who was with child. While they were there, the time came for her to have her child, and she gave birth to her firstborn son. She wrapped him in swaddling clothes and laid him in a manger, because there was no room for them in the inn.

Now there were shepherds in that region living in the fields and keeping the night watch over their flock. The angel of the Lord appeared to them and the glory of the Lord shone around them, and they were struck with great fear. The angel said to them, "Do not be afraid; for behold, I proclaim to you good news of great joy that will be for all the people. For today in the city of David a savior has been born for you who is Christ and Lord.

And this will be a sign for you: you will find an infant wrapped in swaddling clothes and lying in a manger." And suddenly there was a multitude of the heavenly host with the angel, praising God and saying: / "Glory to God in the highest / and on earth peace to those on whom his favor rests."

Brief Silence

For Reflection

Christmas is less about the birth of a baby and far more about the birth of a divine Savior. It is less about glory and joy of long ago and more about an invitation to us today to enter into the saving mystery God revealed so uniquely in Jesus Christ. It is less about drama and more about the nitty-gritty challenge of living daily the mystery of God among us. Christmas is a feast of salvation. This Savior makes for God a new people, those who have been invited into a share of God's glory, God's peace, God's graciousness. Christmas is not a feast for unwrapping earthly gifts; it is a feast for wrapping ourselves in the glory of divine Life brought to us by this Savior Son. Christmas calls us to give the most important gift of all—the very Life of God—to each other. We have been given the Gift of Jesus; now we share this Gift with others as we continue our life journey. Christmas calls us to open our eyes and see where we ourselves can bring the joy and peace of salvation to those around us.

✦ I receive God's message of salvation when . . . through . . . I announce God's message of salvation when . . .

Brief Silence

Prayer

Glorious God, through the birth of your only-begotten Son we receive the gift of a unique communion with you. In the Word made flesh we are given a share in your divine Life. Help us to nurture this great gift of Life until the day when we share everlasting Life with you. We ask this through Christ our Lord. **Amen.**

This feast invites us to reflect on our relationships with God, with each other in our own families, and in the broader family of humanity. During our prayer and reflection let us ask God to make all of us holier and better family members . . .

Prayer

God of love and mercy, justice and righteousness, we come before you mindful that we belong to your holy family, your holy people. May we foster right relationships with others through our good works and grow in our love for you. We ask this through Christ our Lord. **Amen.**

Gospel (Luke 2:22-40)

When the days were completed for their purification according to the law of Moses, they took him up to Jerusalem to present him to the Lord, just as it is written in the law of the Lord, *Every male that opens the womb shall be consecrated to the Lord,* and to offer the sacrifice of *a pair of turtledoves or two young pigeons,* in accordance with the dictate in the law of the Lord.

Now there was a man in Jerusalem whose name was Simeon. This man was righteous and devout, awaiting the consolation of Israel, and the Holy Spirit was upon him. It had been revealed to him by the Holy Spirit that he should not see death before he had seen the Christ of the Lord. He came in the Spirit into the temple; and when the parents brought in the child Jesus to perform the custom of the law in regard to him, he took him into his arms and blessed God, saying: / "Now, Master, you may let your servant go / in peace, according to your word, / for my eyes have seen your salvation, / which you prepared in sight of all the peoples, / a light for revelation to the Gentiles, / and glory for your people Israel." / The child's father and mother were amazed at what was said about him; and Simeon blessed them and said to Mary his mother, "Behold, this child is destined for the fall and rise of many in Israel, and to be a sign that will be contradicted—and you yourself a sword will pierce—so that the thoughts of many hearts may be revealed." There was also a prophetess, Anna, the daughter of Phanuel, of the tribe of Asher. She was advanced in years, having lived seven years with her husband after her marriage, and then as a widow until she was eighty-four. She never left the temple, but worshiped night and day with fasting and prayer. And coming forward at that very time, she gave thanks to God and spoke about the child to all who were awaiting the redemption of Jerusalem.

When they had fulfilled all the prescriptions of the law of the Lord, they returned to Galilee, to their own town of Nazareth. The child grew and became strong, filled with wisdom; and the favor of God was upon him.

Brief Silence

For Reflection

This gospel describes three ways to be righteous. Mary and Joseph bring Jesus to the temple "according to the *law*," fulfilling their obligation as new parents. Simeon is open to the *Holy Spirit's* Presence, guidance, and revelation to him of the "Christ of the Lord." Anna *spoke prophetically* to others about the redemption that was at hand. Faithfulness to the law, openness to the Holy Spirit, prophetically speaking about what has been revealed deepen our right relationship with God. Families are holy when they, too, act righteously as did Mary and Joseph, Simeon, and Anna.

✦ I see the righteousness and holiness in others when I . . . This makes a difference in my ministry because . . .

Brief Silence

Prayer

Triune God, in your very Being you teach us holiness and communion of Persons. May our families be holy and strong, our faithfulness to you and each other sure and true, our righteousness with you and each other grow ever stronger. We ask this through Christ our Lord. **Amen.**

At this time when we celebrate the incarnation of the divine Son, the church gives us this festival to honor Mary, the Mother of God. With her, let us ponder the mystery of God's salvation and open our hearts to receive God's grace during our time of prayer and reflection . . .

Prayer

Gracious God, you chose Mary to be the mother of your divine Son, a woman who said yes to your divine will all the days of her life. Help us to reflect on and ponder your will, so that we remain holy and faithful as Mary. We ask this through Christ our Lord. **Amen.**

Gospel (Luke 2:16-21)

The shepherds went in haste to Bethlehem and found Mary and Joseph, and the infant lying in the manger. When they saw this, they made known the message that had been told them about this child. All who heard it were amazed by what had been told them by the shepherds. And Mary kept all these things, reflecting on them in her heart. Then the shepherds returned, glorifying and praising God for all they had heard and seen, just as it had been told to them.

When eight days were completed for his circumcision, he was named Jesus, the name given him by the angel before he was conceived in the womb.

Brief Silence

For Reflection

Because Mary is the mother of the "infant lying in the manger," she is also the Mother of God. This infant conceived by the Holy Spirit in Mary's womb is both God and man. No doubt Mary reflected "in her heart" on this great mystery throughout her life, a reflection that preserved her as a holy and faithful mother. Our reflection on the mystery of the incarnation must be so deep as Mary's that it brings us to greater holiness and faithfulness. It must bring us, like the shepherds, to come in haste to encounter the One who deserves all glory and praise.

Honoring Mary as the Mother of God goes beyond the event of her giving birth to the Son of God. By keeping "all these things" and "reflecting on them in her heart," she exhibits a life of encountering God and being open to whatever God asks of her. Like Mary, we must ponder God's entry into our own lives, making the divine Presence the very "stuff" of our hearts.

✦ Those things I keep in my heart and reflect upon are . . .

Brief Silence

Prayer

O God who deserves all glory and praise, may we come to you in haste with hearts filled with awe at the great mystery of Mary being chosen to be the mother of your divine Son. Help us to imitate her holiness and one day share with her in the fullness of Life you offer those who are faithful. We ask this through Christ our Lord. **Amen.**

The magi were guided by the light of God's star to the newborn King. We pause to reflect on how we have sometimes failed to recognize God's light guiding us . . .

Prayer

God of light and darkness, you created this world filled with contrasts that invite us to choose you as our only good. Inspire us to seek the change in our lives that brings us ever closer to the light of your only-begotten Son, living in his goodness and mercy all the days of our lives. We ask this through Christ our Lord. **Amen.**

Gospel **(Matt 2:1-12)**

When Jesus was born in Bethlehem of Judea, in the days of King Herod, behold, magi from the east arrived in Jerusalem, saying, "Where is the newborn king of the Jews? We saw his star at its rising and have come to do him homage." When King Herod heard this, he was greatly troubled, and all Jerusalem with him. Assembling all the chief priests and the scribes of the people, he inquired of them where the Christ was to be born. They said to him, "In Bethlehem of Judea, for thus it has been written through the prophet: / *And you, Bethlehem, land of Judah, / are by no means least among the rulers of Judah; / since from you shall come a ruler, / who is to shepherd my people Israel." /* Then Herod called the magi secretly and ascertained from them the time of the star's appearance. He sent them to Bethlehem and said, "Go and search diligently for the child. When you have found him, bring me word, that I too may go and do him homage." After their audience with the king they set out. And behold, the star that they had seen at its rising preceded them, until it came and stopped over the place where the child was. They were overjoyed at seeing the star, and on entering the house they saw the child with Mary his mother. They prostrated themselves and did him homage. Then they opened their treasures and offered him gifts of gold, frankincense, and myrrh. And having been warned in a dream not to return to Herod, they departed for their country by another way.

Brief Silence

For Reflection

This gospel uncovers a number of contrasts: the magi-Gentiles from the east vs. Herod and the Jews of all Jerusalem; the light of the star that guided the magi vs. the darkness of Herod's heart; the "newborn king of the Jews" thought to be found in Jerusalem, the home of Israel's king vs. this Child being found in the small village of Bethlehem; Herod breeding evil in his heart to keep his power and status vs. the magi who paid homage and offered gifts to the Child. Searching for and finding the Christ necessitates a choice in face of contrasts: to accept or reject this new in-breaking of God. Further, there can be no encounter with Christ without a change in us. The Light of Christ changes us because it opens up for us a divine world we cannot imagine but is so attractive that we let go of self in order to allow God to fashion us in this Light that never fades. The magi followed the light, encountered the Light, offered homage to the Light. So must we.

✦ The contrasts I encounter in my daily living are . . . The choices I make in face of them are . . .

Brief Silence

Prayer

May our Holy Communion, O God, strengthen us to be sure in the choices we make to live a good life. May we encounter the light of Christ among us and offer homage and praise to you for such a wondrous gift. We ask this through Christ our Lord. **Amen.**

On this feast day we celebrate Jesus' baptism in the Jordan when the heavens were opened, the Spirit descended, and he was revealed as God's beloved Son. We also celebrate the grace of our own baptism and identity as God's daughters and sons. During our prayer let us reflect on our own baptismal faithfulness and God's great gift of Life given to us . . .

Prayer

God of life and love, you invite us through our baptism in the Holy Spirit to become your beloved daughters and sons in whom you are well pleased. Help us to be faithful to our baptismal promises and the identity of being members of the Body of Christ you have so graciously bestowed upon us. We ask this through Christ our Lord. **Amen.**

Gospel (Mark 1:7-11)

This is what John the Baptist proclaimed: "One mightier than I is coming after me. I am not worthy to stoop and loosen the thongs of his sandals. I have baptized you with water; he will baptize you with the Holy Spirit."

It happened in those days that Jesus came from Nazareth of Galilee and was baptized in the Jordan by John. On coming up out of the water he saw the heavens being torn open and the Spirit, like a dove, descending upon him. And a voice came from the heavens, "You are my beloved Son; with you I am well pleased."

Brief Silence

For Reflection

The event of Jesus' baptism with water in the Jordan revealed who he already was: the "beloved Son" with whom God was "well pleased." Jesus' baptism did not change his identity, but revealed who he was. John prophesied that Jesus, however, would bring an entirely different baptism, for he would baptize us with the Holy Spirit. The event of our baptism with the Spirit announces to all present who we become: beloved children with whom God is "well pleased." Baptism initiates us into a way of living defined by a relationship of identity. Our whole Christian life is a journey of taking ownership of the ownership God has already taken of us. Through baptism God claims us. Through baptism we become one with Christ. An essential tenet of Christianity is that baptism plunges us into an ongoing way of living whereby our lives are patterned after Christ's. By the indwelling of the Spirit we become adopted sons and daughters of God, God's "beloved," too. By this indwelling—God's very Life—Jesus' life and way of living becomes our own. Jesus' saving work becomes our own life work.

✦ My manner of distributing Communion helps the communicants take ownership of who they are as God's beloved when . . .

Brief Silence

Prayer

May this Holy Communion, gracious God, nurture us in the way of living to which our baptism calls us. May we be faithful to living the Gospel and one day come to share in the fullness of Life you promise those who never swerve from your divine will and love. We ask this through Christ our Lord. **Amen.**

Just as Jesus called Andrew and Peter and the other disciples, he calls each of us to be his followers. As we begin this time of prayer and reflection, let us ask ourselves how faithfully we have followed Jesus . . .

Prayer

Loving God, you sent your Son to dwell among us, to be our gentle Lamb of God, to show us a life of total self-giving. May we behold this Lamb of God among us and within us and follow him faithfully, no matter what the cost. We ask this through Christ our Lord. **Amen.**

Gospel (John 1:35-42)

John was standing with two of his disciples, and as he watched Jesus walk by, he said, "Behold, the Lamb of God." The two disciples heard what he said and followed Jesus. Jesus turned and saw them following him and said to them, "What are you looking for?" They said to him, "Rabbi"—which translated means Teacher—, "where are you staying?" He said to them, "Come, and you will see." So they went and saw where Jesus was staying, and they stayed with him that day. It was about four in the afternoon. Andrew, the brother of Simon Peter, was one of the two who heard John and followed Jesus. He first found his own brother Simon and told him, "We have found the Messiah"—which is translated Christ. Then he brought him to Jesus. Jesus looked at him and said, "You are Simon the son of John; you will be called Cephas"—which is translated Peter.

Brief Silence

For Reflection

The two disciples in this gospel would have interpreted John the Baptist's cry, "Behold, the Lamb of God," within the Passover and temple tradition of sacrifice of lambs. What is startling about John's cry is that he uses this sacrificial reference not for a lamb, an animal, but for a human being who was walking by—Jesus. John is pointing to Jesus as the One who will be sacrificed. Little did they know at this point that the core of following Jesus is sacrifice—a total self-giving. Still, they followed him. As with all disciples, it took a time of rubbing shoulders with Jesus, hearing him teach and preach, observing his interactions with people, observing him pray, experiencing his resoluteness about his mission for them to begin to know Jesus, grasp his mission, and absorb the strength and courage to live his total self-giving life. Growing in total self-giving takes much time, and is absolutely essential for anyone who claims to be a disciple of Jesus. We are able to follow Jesus' example of total self-sacrifice only when we "Behold" him, when we keep our eyes focused on him and his Good News of salvation.

✦ My distributing Holy Communion helps me understand better that Mass calls me to greater self-giving when . . .

Brief Silence

Prayer

Our Holy Communion, almighty God, gives us a share in Christ's life and draws us into his self-giving. May our lives reflect his goodness, our hopes be fulfilled, and our faith grow strong as we live the Gospel. We ask this through Christ our Lord. **Amen.**

In this gospel Jesus calls disciples to follow him in his work of salvation. We pause at the beginning of our prayer and reflection to hear Jesus' call to us and consider how well we have responded . . .

Prayer

You call us, O God of salvation, to continue your divine Son's mission to our world and bring everyone to a time of fulfillment. Open us to hear your call in our daily lives and strengthen us to answer with the strength of our convictions and the goodness of our lives. We ask this through Christ our Lord. **Amen.**

Gospel (Mark 1:14-20)

After John had been arrested, Jesus came to Galilee proclaiming the gospel of God: "This is the time of fulfillment. The kingdom of God is at hand. Repent, and believe in the gospel."

As he passed by the Sea of Galilee, he saw Simon and his brother Andrew casting their nets into the sea; they were fishermen. Jesus said to them, "Come after me, and I will make you fishers of men." Then they abandoned their nets and followed him. He walked along a little farther and saw James, the son of Zebedee, and his brother John. They too were in a boat mending their nets. Then he called them. So they left their father Zebedee in the boat along with the hired men and followed him.

Brief Silence

For Reflection

We hear in this gospel a call to "come after" Jesus. Following Jesus requires change, whether that be the radical one of leaving all to follow Jesus, or the more modest one of turning from the little everyday behaviors that cause us to focus on ourselves and our own needs rather than on Jesus and the needs of others. This means, of course, that this kind of change required for discipleship always has a cost. Hearing Jesus' call to discipleship and choosing to follow him faithfully literally assures us we will meet adversity and suffering, as did both John and Jesus. The surprise of the gospel is not that we will face adversity, however. The surprise is that in preaching repentance and changing our lives, "the time of fulfillment" is upon us. This gospel is a call-response episode where the call comes within the context of Jesus' proclamation that now is "the time of fulfillment." "The kingdom of God is at hand" in Jesus who manifests God's abiding Presence, God's promise of forgiveness, God's unparalleled power to save. To enter into this "time of fulfillment," we must leave everything behind and answer Jesus' call to follow him.

✦ Holy Communion is a "time of fulfillment" for me . . . for those coming to Holy Communion . . .

Brief Silence

Prayer

O God, in the gift of Holy Communion we experience the pledge of fullness of Life with you. May we ever grow in our thanksgiving for your great gift, and offer ourselves as living sacrifices for the good of all. We ask this through Christ our Lord. **Amen.**

In this gospel, Jesus acts with the authority of holiness to banish an unclean spirit. As we spend time in prayer and reflection, let us acknowledge our need for Jesus to banish the unclean spirits in our own lives . . .

Prayer

God of might and power, your authority is the origin of all life and holiness. May we hear Jesus' teaching with authority with open hearts and learn to follow him more diligently, bringing new life to all we meet. We ask this through Christ our Lord. **Amen.**

Gospel (Mark 1:21-28)

Then they came to Capernaum, and on the sabbath Jesus entered the synagogue and taught. The people were astonished at his teaching, for he taught them as one having authority and not as the scribes. In their synagogue was a man with an unclean spirit; he cried out, "What have you to do with us, Jesus of Nazareth? Have you come to destroy us? I know who you are—the Holy One of God!" Jesus rebuked him and said, "Quiet! Come out of him!" The unclean spirit convulsed him and with a loud cry came out of him. All were amazed and asked one another, "What is this? A new teaching with authority. He commands even the unclean spirits and they obey him." His fame spread everywhere through-out the whole region of Galilee.

Brief Silence

For Reflection

This gospel narrates the first of many dramatic confrontations between holiness and evil. Banishing evil is the work of salvation Jesus has been sent to do, and he does so with authority. He has this authority because he is "the Holy One of God." Holiness is "of God"; evil is everything that is opposed to God.

In the gospel, Jesus' "authority" is not perceived as a negative power over, as the ability to control others. Jesus' authority rests in the meaning of the word itself; from the Latin, *auctor*, "authority" refers to origin, originator. Jesus has authority not simply because he is "of God," but because he *is* God, the origin of all authority, goodness, and truth. Jesus' authority ushers forth from who he is: God, the originator of all life and holiness. Jesus' authority rests in his identity as the divine Son. The "new teaching with authority" about which the people are amazed is not the healing miracle in itself, but rather the display of God's face-to-face Presence mediated in Jesus. Jesus is the authority of holiness incarnate.

✦ Jesus speaks to me with authority about . . . He gives me authority to . . .

Brief Silence

Prayer

Holy God, our participation in the sacrament of the Holy Eucharist strengthens us to overcome evil, grants us the holiness of your divine Life, and gifts us with the authority to bring that Life to others. May we be ever faithful to this precious gift of love so generously given us. We ask this through Christ our Lord. **Amen.**

The purpose for which Jesus came among us was to preach the Good News and heal human suffering. As we begin our time of prayer and reflection, let us acknowledge the times when we have failed to preach the Good News by our lives and open ourselves to hear God's word anew . . .

Prayer

As the people in the gospel were looking for Jesus, we pray, O God, that we might also be diligent in looking for him and opening ourselves to the healing and salvation he so faithfully offers us. May we never lose sight of Jesus as the One who brings us all good things. We ask this through Christ our Lord. **Amen.**

Gospel (Mark 1:29-39)

On leaving the synagogue Jesus entered the house of Simon and Andrew with James and John. Simon's mother-in-law lay sick with a fever. They immediately told him about her. He approached, grasped her hand, and helped her up. Then the fever left her and she waited on them.

When it was evening, after sunset, they brought to him all who were ill or possessed by demons. The whole town was gathered at the door. He cured many who were sick with various diseases, and he drove out many demons, not permitting them to speak because they knew him.

Rising very early before dawn, he left and went off to a deserted place, where he prayed. Simon and those who were with him pursued him and on finding him said, "Everyone is looking for you." He told them, "Let us go on to the nearby villages that I may preach there also. For this purpose have I come." So he went into their synagogues, preaching and driving out demons throughout the whole of Galilee.

Brief Silence

For Reflection

In the gospel Simon says to Jesus, "Everyone is looking for you." Jesus is having great success healing many people and driving out demons. People are paying great attention to him—"The whole town was gathered" at the door of Simon and Andrew's house. Nonetheless, Jesus moves on to other villages. Personal idolization is not the purpose for which Jesus has come. His ministry is not about drawing attention to himself, but about preaching the Good News of salvation. Yet his ministry *is* about himself, for he *is* the Good News. His ministry is about reaching out to others and easing their burdens of life. And so he cures those brought to him who are "ill or possessed by demons." But his ministry is more than this. His ministry is about helping others move beyond their immediate life concerns to reach for the Life he offers them. The healing is the medium for calling the people to a renewed relationship with God. In the midst of attention and adulation by the people for what he is doing, Jesus never loses sight of his mission to bring a deeper healing to everyone.

✦ My acclamation "Body of Christ" or "Blood of Christ" preaches the Good News of salvation in that . . .

Brief Silence

Prayer

Healing God, you see into our hearts and know that we need to hear the Good News and come to the salvation you offer us. Help us to hear with open ears, to receive with loving hearts, and to live with passion and compassion. We ask this through Christ our Lord. **Amen.**

In this gospel, Jesus does more than heal a leper. By stretching out his hand and touching him, Jesus restores his dignity as a person. Let us pause to call to mind the times we have failed to treat others with dignity . . .

Prayer

Gracious God, you kindly bestow upon us a new dignity as, through our baptism, we are grafted onto Christ. May we cherish our own dignity and respond compassionately to the dignity of others. We ask this through Christ our Lord. **Amen.**

Gospel (Mark 1:40-45)

A leper came to Jesus and kneeling down begged him and said, "If you wish, you can make me clean." Moved with pity, he stretched out his hand, touched him, and said to him, "I do will it. Be made clean." The leprosy left him immediately, and he was made clean. Then, warning him sternly, he dismissed him at once.

He said to him, "See that you tell no one anything, but go, show yourself to the priest and offer for your cleansing what Moses prescribed; that will be proof for them."

The man went away and began to publicize the whole matter. He spread the report abroad so that it was impossible for Jesus to enter a town openly. He remained outside in deserted places, and people kept coming to him from everywhere.

Brief Silence

For Reflection

The leper in the gospel, excluded from the community and well aware of his miserable plight, understandably approached Jesus with caution ("If you wish") and humility ("kneeling down"). Jesus, however, has no doubt about his response, for his purpose in coming among us was to show the compassion of God for the outcast: "I do will it." Jesus' compassion gave the leper what he deeply wished—to be made clean, yes, but also once again to be restored to relations that were lost, to have a life other than one determined by pain, to have an opportunity for a different outlook on death. This healing account between a leper and Jesus dramatically unfolds in a conversation punctuated by concrete and very personal gestures. The leper comes to Jesus, kneels, and boldly begs for cleansing, gestures expressing his sense of unworthiness. Moved with pity, Jesus stretches out his hand and touches the leper, gestures revealing the leper's inherent dignity. Jesus heals more than the man's body. Encounter with Jesus and being healed always fashions a new relationship with him. Freed from pain and isolation, the leper can let his inherent dignity spill over into proclaiming the Good News of a new Presence, a new Awakening, a new Life.

✦ When I see the inherent dignity of each person coming to receive Holy Communion, my ministry becomes . . .

Brief Silence

Prayer

Compassionate God, your Son's gift of his Body and Blood raises us up to a share in the new Life of the resurrection. May we always have grateful hearts for the great dignity of Life and holiness we receive. We ask this through Christ our Lord. **Amen.**

As we begin our yearly observance of Lent, let us reflect on how we have grown during the past year and acknowledge where we have failed to live up to our baptismal commitment . . .

Prayer

We begin Lent, O God, not with hearts dreading penance but with a spirit of expectation of the grace to change what takes us from growing in right relationship with you and others. May our penance be fruitful and our expectations be fulfilled. We ask this through Christ our Lord. **Amen.**

Gospel (Matt 6:1-6, 16-18)

Jesus said to his disciples: "Take care not to perform righteous deeds in order that people may see them; otherwise, you will have no recompense from your heavenly Father. When you give alms, do not blow a trumpet before you, as the hypocrites do in the synagogues and in the streets to win the praise of others. Amen, I say to you, they have received their reward. But when you give alms, do not let your left hand know what your right is doing, so that your almsgiving may be secret. And your Father who sees in secret will repay you.

"When you pray, do not be like the hypocrites, who love to stand and pray in the synagogues and on street corners so that others may see them. Amen, I say to you, they have received their reward. But when you pray, go to your inner room, close the door, and pray to your Father in secret. And your Father who sees in secret will repay you.

"When you fast, do not look gloomy like the hypocrites. They neglect their appearance, so that they may appear to others to be fasting. Amen, I say to you, they have received their reward. But when you fast, anoint your head and wash your face, so that you may not appear to be fasting, except to your Father who is hidden. And your Father who sees what is hidden will repay you."

Brief Silence

For Reflection

The opening line of the gospel mentions "righteous deeds." In a biblical context, "righteous deeds" are those which have to do with relationships; they are any acts which help us relate to others with the same care and goodness with which God relates to us. One is "righteous" when one is "right" with God and others, as expressed in our concrete behaviors. On the surface, it's a little difficult not to get the point of this gospel: don't do spiritual acts—no matter how good and worthy they are—so that others see them and think well of us. Three times in this gospel Jesus tells us to do "righteous deeds" not to be noticed by others, but to be repaid by God. God's "repayment" is nothing less than a deepened relationship with God. This gospel is essentially a reminder of the work of Lent: to make God the center of our lives. The regard and praise of others is not what we seek, but a deeper love relationship with the God who is "gracious and merciful."

✦ To persevere in my chosen Lenten penance and thus form a new habit of righteous living, I must . . .

Brief Silence

Prayer

May Holy Communion increase in us, O God, our desire to live as your beloved daughters and sons, marked by good practices of prayer, fasting, and charity. Strengthen us for our Lenten task and one day bring us to the fullness of Life with you. We ask this through Christ our Lord. **Amen.**

The gospel account invites us to go off to a deserted place to confront our temptations and to repent and believe the Gospel. We pause to repent of the times we have given in to temptation and failed to live the Gospel . . .

Prayer

God of Good News, during this Lent bring us to greater belief and deeper repentance for our wrongdoing. May we turn our lives more completely toward you and your goodness, thus witnessing to how the Gospel of your divine Son has taken root within us. We ask this through Christ our Lord. **Amen.**

Gospel (Mark 1:12-15)

The Spirit drove Jesus out into the desert, and he remained in the desert for forty days, tempted by Satan. He was among wild beasts, and the angels ministered to him.

After John had been arrested, Jesus came to Galilee proclaiming the gospel of God: "This is the time of fulfillment. The kingdom of God is at hand. Repent, and believe in the gospel."

Brief Silence

For Reflection

Mark's version of the temptation in the desert is short and to the point. He does not relay the details of Jesus' experience of temptation, but he does show its outcome: Jesus boldly enters Galilee proclaiming, "This is the time . . . Repent, and believe." Temptations always force us to make a choice. Jesus' choice is to take up his saving mission. What is our temptation? What is our choice? These are *the* questions of Lent. They are the questions those of us who are baptized into Christ must constantly ask if we wish to participate in his saving mission, proclaiming by the choices we make that the Gospel determines who we are and how we act.

Confronting temptation and overcoming the sinfulness that keeps us from righteous Christian living is a necessary first step for faithful baptismal living. We must turn from sinfulness before we can do our part to continue Jesus' mission. We do so by proclaiming the Gospel, which is a lifelong mission. The most eloquent proclamation of the Gospel is the witness of the way we live. Ultimately, what we witness to is the "time of fulfillment" brought about by believing in and living the Gospel.

✦ The manner in which I distribute Holy Communion strengthens the community's belief in the "gospel of God" when I . . .

Brief Silence

Prayer

Though we are tempted, O God, to make wrong choices during our daily living, we beg you to strengthen us for Gospel living and fidelity to our baptismal commitment. May our Lenten penance be fruitful during this time of repentance. We ask this through Christ our Lord. **Amen.**

Jesus' transfiguration gives us a glimpse of the glory that awaits us when we, too, die to self for the sake of others. Let us take some time to examine when we have put ourselves ahead of God and others and ask for God's mercy . . .

Prayer

Saving God, the mystery of your Son become incarnate never ceases to reveal to us ever anew who Jesus is for us. Help us to see ever more clearly his risen Presence among us and to live the Gospel in such a way that we, too, become theophanies of his Body among us. We ask this through Christ our Lord. **Amen.**

Gospel **(Mark 9:2-10)**

Jesus took Peter, James, and John and led them up a high mountain apart by themselves. And he was transfigured before them, and his clothes became dazzling white, such as no fuller on earth could bleach them. Then Elijah appeared to them along with Moses, and they were conversing with Jesus. Then Peter said to Jesus in reply, "Rabbi, it is good that we are here! Let us make three tents: one for you, one for Moses, and one for Elijah." He hardly knew what to say, they were so terrified. Then a cloud came, casting a shadow over them; from the cloud came a voice, "This is my beloved Son. Listen to him." Suddenly, looking around, they no longer saw anyone but Jesus alone with them.

As they were coming down from the mountain, he charged them not to relate what they had seen to anyone, except when the Son of Man had risen from the dead. So they kept the matter to themselves, questioning what rising from the dead meant.

Brief Silence

For Reflection

On the mountain Peter, James, and John witness the first three theophanies (manifestations of divine Presence): Jesus the transfigured One, Jesus the "beloved Son," Jesus the "Son of Man." As the transfigured One, Jesus reveals what is yet to come. As the "beloved Son," the Father reveals an intimate, divine relationship. As the "Son of Man," Jesus reveals that he is the new Israel (see Dan 7:13-14), the Messiah who would bring salvation. All three of these theophanies, these revelations of who Jesus is, point to something entirely new happening. But to embrace the new has its cost.

Coming "down from the mountain," Peter, James, and John would witness Jesus passing through death to the full revelation of what had been foreshadowed in his transfiguration: the theophany of his risen, glorified Body. This is a whole new Presence of the divine in our midst, a risen One who would never again face death. Finally, when Peter, James, and John choose dying to self, they are transfigured by Jesus' risen Life. *They* too become theophanies. So can *we*.

✦ I am a theophany when I . . . Others who have been a theophany for me are . . .

Brief Silence

Prayer

Loving God, you manifest your Son's love and continual self-giving in the gift of the Eucharist which we share. May this wondrous theophany of divine Presence nourish us to live faithfully the Gospel of self-giving he taught us and one day bring us to the fullness of Life we receive. We ask this through Christ our Lord. **Amen.**

In this Sunday's gospel we hear the account of Jesus cleansing the temple. Let us reflect during our prayer on what needs to be cleansed from the temple of our own hearts . . .

Prayer

In due season, O God, you fashion us into temples of your divine Son's risen Presence. May our faithfulness to his Gospel become a living sign of his desire for our salvation. We ask this through Christ our Lord. **Amen.**

Gospel (John 2:13-25)

Since the Passover of the Jews was near, Jesus went up to Jerusalem. He found in the temple area those who sold oxen, sheep, and doves, as well as the money changers seated there. He made a whip out of cords and drove them all out of the temple area, with the sheep and oxen, and spilled the coins of the money changers and overturned their tables, and to those who sold doves he said, "Take these out of here, and stop making my Father's house a marketplace." His disciples recalled the words of Scripture, *Zeal for your house will consume me.* At this the Jews answered and said to him, "What sign can you show us for doing this?" Jesus answered and said to them, "Destroy this temple and in three days I will raise it up." The Jews said, "This temple has been under construction for forty-six years, and you will raise it up in three days?" But he was speaking about the temple of his body. Therefore, when he was raised from the dead, his disciples remembered that he had said this, and they came to believe the Scripture and the word Jesus had spoken.

While he was in Jerusalem for the feast of Passover, many began to believe in his name when they saw the signs he was doing. But Jesus would not trust himself to them because he knew them all, and did not need anyone to testify about human nature. He himself understood it well.

Brief Silence

For Reflection

The temple in Jerusalem was a sign to the Jews of God's Presence and saving works. This sign could be corrupted, however, by human beings who turn away from the temple's true purpose. Enraged, Jesus takes "a whip" and drives out of the temple area those who corrupt the sign. Then Jesus announces both a new temple (his own body) that could not be corrupted and a new sign ("raised from the dead") that would draw those who come to believe in him to a whole new reality. Even though the new temple of Jesus' body would be destroyed by death, in the end it was not. This temple would be an eternal sign of God's Presence and saving works and those who wish to share in Jesus' Life cannot lose sight of this sign. God's Presence and saving works are not found in bricks and mortar, but in the risen Body of Christ. Now *we* are the new temple: the living sign of the new things God is doing for us. This living sign is no longer a place (a bricks and mortar temple), but a relationship of fidelity to a new temple (the risen Jesus).

✦ My manner of distributing Holy Communion reveals my reverence for the communicants as temples of God's Presence when I . . .

Brief Silence

Prayer

In a temple of bricks and mortar we receive, gracious God, the gift of your divine Son's Body and Blood. This gift transforms us into living signs of his Presence and pledges to us the fullness of Life with you. May we be ever grateful for this gift and pledge. We ask this through Christ our Lord. **Amen.**

The gospel this Sunday challenges us to believe in Jesus and choose light over darkness. For the times when we have chosen the darkness of sin, let us ask for God's mercy and forgiveness . . .

Prayer

We plead, merciful God, for your mercy as we work out in our lives the salvation you offer us. Strengthen us to be self-giving by faithfully doing the work that the Gospel demands. We ask this through Christ our Lord. **Amen.**

Gospel (John 3:14-21)

Jesus said to Nicodemus: "Just as Moses lifted up the serpent in the desert, so must the Son of Man be lifted up, so that everyone who believes in him may have eternal life."

For God so loved the world that he gave his only Son, so that everyone who believes in him might not perish but might have eternal life. For God did not send his Son into the world to condemn the world, but that the world might be saved through him. Whoever believes in him will not be condemned, but whoever does not believe has already been condemned, because he has not believed in the name of the only Son of God. And this is the verdict, that the light came into the world, but people preferred darkness to light, because their works were evil. For everyone who does wicked things hates the light and does not come toward the light, so that his works might not be exposed. But whoever lives the truth comes to the light, so that his works may be clearly seen as done in God.

Brief Silence

For Reflection

There are two parts to this gospel, separated by the line "And this is the verdict." The first part concerns the evidence: God "gave his only Son" in whom we choose to believe or not. The second part gives the judgment: those are saved who believe in Jesus, live the truth, and come to the light. Those are condemned who do not believe in Jesus, prefer darkness, and do "wicked things." Our whole life is working out our own verdict. Thank God we are at the mercy of a gracious and forgiving God!

God's work is this: to die to self so that we can be raised to new life. God demonstrates great love for us by giving the Son to be lifted up on the cross and then raised to eternal Life and glory. We demonstrate our great love for God by doing the work of God— dying and rising, conforming ourselves so completely to Christ that we cooperate in his very work of salvation. We need not fear the verdict of God's judgment at the end of our lives if we daily work at increasing the depth of our believing and Gospel living.

✦ My choosing to believe in Jesus is reflected in the way I minister Holy Communion in that . . .

Brief Silence

Prayer

Merciful and forgiving God, by our Holy Communion may we commit ourselves to our Lenten penance with hearts turned to you. Help us to live the Gospel in such a way that we fear not your judgment, but look forward with grateful hearts to the fullness of Life you offer those who are faithful. We ask this through Christ our Lord. **Amen.**

The gospel calls us to be grains of wheat that die to bear fruit, to lose life to find new life, and to follow Jesus faithfully. Let us empty ourselves of anything that keeps us from dying to self and beg God's forgiveness and mercy for the times when we have failed . . .

Prayer

Our lives are filled with suffering, O God, and we seek mercy and relief. Help us to see beyond our daily suffering to the glory of new Life that faithfully following your Son's Gospel way of living brings. We ask this through Christ our Lord. **Amen.**

Gospel (John 12:20-33)

Some Greeks who had come to worship at the Passover Feast came to Philip, who was from Bethsaida in Galilee, and asked him, "Sir, we would like to see Jesus." Philip went and told Andrew; then Andrew and Philip went and told Jesus. Jesus answered them, "The hour has come for the Son of Man to be glorified. Amen, amen, I say to you, unless a grain of wheat falls to the ground and dies, it remains just a grain of wheat; but if it dies, it produces much fruit. Whoever loves his life loses it, and whoever hates his life in this world will preserve it for eternal life. Whoever serves me must follow me, and where I am, there also will my servant be. The Father will honor whoever serves me.

"I am troubled now. Yet what should I say? 'Father, save me from this hour'? But it was for this purpose that I came to this hour. Father, glorify your name." Then a voice came from heaven, "I have glorified it and will glorify it again." The crowd there heard it and said it was thunder; but others said, "An angel has spoken to him." Jesus answered and said, "This voice did not come for my sake but for yours. Now is the time of judgment on this world; now the ruler of this world will be driven out. And when I am lifted up from the earth, I will draw everyone to myself." He said this indicating the kind of death he would die.

Brief Silence

For Reflection

In this gospel Jesus speaks of different kinds of pain. There is the physical pain of his crucifixion, alluded to when he speaks of his being "lifted up from the earth." He also speaks of the pain of dying, of losing our life, of serving him by following him. In all this pain, the focus is not on the suffering, but on the fruits that come from being faithful. The dying grain "produces much fruit"; losing one's life now "preserves it for eternal life"; serving brings "honor."

Jesus reveals his "hour . . . to be glorified" in surprisingly inglorious ways: dying grain, losing life, serving others. When we focus only on the pain of giving up and the giving over of our lives, we fail to take into account the glorification. By Jesus giving his life over for our salvation, glorification bursts forth. The Father is glorified in the very giving over of the Son. The Son is glorified in giving himself over to the cross. We are glorified in giving ourselves over to following Jesus to the cross. And this glorification is fullness of Life.

✦ Some ways that I might manifest the Eucharist as both the suffering of the cross and the glory of the Resurrection are . . .

Brief Silence

Prayer

God of the cross and resurrection, you ever beckon us to the glory of new Life. May we willingly give ourselves over to following Jesus to the cross, and one day share in the fullness of his glory in everlasting Life. We ask this through Christ our Lord. **Amen.**

As we begin this solemn Holy Week with sincere prayer, we pause to reflect on our willingness to follow Jesus in times of glory, and our unwillingness to follow him when carrying the cross . . .

Prayer

Merciful God, you are ever near even when we turn away from you and sin. Encourage us by your loving Presence so that we might stand faithfully with Jesus by living the Gospel daily without hesitation or fear. We ask this through Christ our Lord. **Amen.**

Gospel (Mark 15:1-39)

As soon as morning came, the chief priests with the elders and the scribes, that is, the whole Sanhedrin held a council. They bound Jesus, led him away, and handed him over to Pilate. Pilate questioned him, "Are you the king of the Jews?" He said to him in reply, "You say so." The chief priests accused him of many things. Again Pilate questioned him, "Have you no answer? See how many things they accuse you of." Jesus gave him no further answer, so that Pilate was amazed.

Now on the occasion of the feast he used to release to them one prisoner whom they requested. A man called Barabbas was then in prison along with the rebels who had committed murder in a rebellion. The crowd came forward and began to ask him to do for them as he was accustomed. Pilate answered, "Do you want me to release to you the king of the Jews?" For he knew that it was out of envy that the chief priests had handed him over. But the chief priests stirred up the crowd to have him release Barabbas for them instead. Pilate again said to them in reply, "Then what do you want me to do with the man you call the king of the Jews?" They shouted again, "Crucify him." Pilate said to them, "Why? What evil has he done?" They only shouted the louder, "Crucify him." So Pilate, wishing to satisfy the crowd, released Barabbas to them and, after he had Jesus scourged, handed him over to be crucified.

The soldiers led him away inside the palace, that is, the praetorium, and assembled the whole cohort. They clothed him in purple and, weaving a crown of thorns, placed it on him. They began to salute him with, "Hail, King of the Jews!" and kept striking his head with a reed and spitting upon him. They knelt before him in homage. And when they had mocked him, they stripped him of the purple cloak, dressed him in his own clothes, and led him out to crucify him.

They pressed into service a passer-by, Simon, a Cyrenian, who was coming in from the country, the father of Alexander and Rufus, to carry his cross.

They brought him to the place of Golgotha—which is translated Place of the Skull—. They gave him wine drugged with myrrh, but he did not take it. Then they crucified him and divided his garments by casting lots for them to see what each should take. It was nine o'clock in the morning when they crucified him. The inscription of the charge against him read, "The King of the Jews." With him they crucified two revolutionaries, one on his right and one on his left. Those passing by reviled him, shaking their heads and saying, "Aha! You who would destroy the temple and rebuild it in three days, save yourself by coming down from the cross." Likewise the chief priests, with the scribes, mocked him among themselves and said, "He saved others; he cannot save himself. Let the Christ, the King of Israel, come down now from the cross that we may see and believe." Those who were crucified with him also kept abusing him.

At noon darkness came over the whole land until three in the afternoon. And at three o'clock Jesus cried out in a loud voice, *"Eloi, Eloi, lema sabachthani?"* which is translated, "My God, my God, why have you forsaken me?" Some of the bystanders who heard it said, "Look, he is calling Elijah." One of them ran, soaked a sponge with wine, put it on a reed and gave it to him to drink saying, "Wait, let us see if Elijah comes to take him down." Jesus gave a loud cry and breathed his last.

The veil of the sanctuary was torn in two from top to bottom. When the centurion who stood facing him saw how he breathed his last he said, "Truly this man was the Son of God!"

Brief Silence

For Reflection

In Mark's account of Jesus' passion, many persons respond to Jesus in many different ways. A woman anoints him with perfumed oil, anticipating his burial. At the Last Supper, Peter and the rest of the Twelve swear they will never deny him. In Gethsemane, the apostles sleep. Judas betrays Jesus with a kiss. In fear, a young man runs away naked (really fast!). During the trial, many give false witness. Peter denies Jesus three times. Pilate hands him over to be crucified. Soldiers mock him. Simon of Cyrene helps him carry the cross. Soldiers crucify him. The centurion proclaims Jesus to be the "Son of God." At the crucifixion, many women remained present. Joseph of Arimathea buries Jesus. During Jesus' last hours, only a few faithful people stand by Jesus. Most do not. As we hear this passion proclaimed, where do we stand? Our call as we hear this passion account proclaimed and embrace more fully our baptismal commitment is to stand with Jesus, to become so one with him that our denials become fewer, our running from him becomes less quick, our faithfulness to following him and continuing his mission becomes stronger.

✦ I stand by Jesus when . . .

Brief Silence

Prayer

Loving God, each day you kiss us with your divine Presence and gift us with the nourishment of the Body and Blood of your divine Son. Help us to stand firmly on the foundation of your Presence and never stray from the Life you offer us. We ask this through Christ our Lord. **Amen.**

On Holy Thursday we remember Jesus' self-giving love in offering us his Body and Blood for nourishment. We remember his modeling for us how we are to give our lives in service. Let us enter into this great mystery of love . . .

Prayer

We naturally turn away from sacrificial self-giving, loving God, to satisfy our own wants and desires. May we learn from Jesus' actions at this Last Supper with his disciples to be as caring and giving as he was. May we give ourselves to others as he did. We ask this through Christ our Lord. **Amen.**

Gospel (John 13:1-15)

Before the feast of Passover, Jesus knew that his hour had come to pass from this world to the Father. He loved his own in the world and he loved them to the end. The devil had already induced Judas, son of Simon the Iscariot, to hand him over. So, during supper, fully aware that the Father had put everything into his power and that he had come from God and was returning to God, he rose from supper and took off his outer garments. He took a towel and tied it around his waist. Then he poured water into a basin and began to wash the disciples' feet and dry them with the towel around his waist. He came to Simon Peter, who said to him, "Master, are you going to wash my feet?" Jesus answered and said to him, "What I am doing, you do not understand now, but you will understand later." Peter said to him, "You will never wash my feet." Jesus answered him, "Unless I wash you, you will have no inheritance with me." Simon Peter said to him, "Master, then not only my feet, but my hands and head as well." Jesus said to him, "Whoever has bathed has no need except to have his feet washed, for he is clean all over; so you are clean, but not all." For he knew who would betray him; for this reason, he said, "Not all of you are clean."

So when he had washed their feet and put his garments back on and reclined at table again, he said to them, "Do you realize what I have done for you? You call me 'teacher' and 'master,' and rightly so, for indeed I am. If I, therefore, the master and teacher, have washed your feet, you ought to wash one another's feet. I have given you a model to follow, so that as I have done for you, you should also do."

Brief Silence

For Reflection

This night Jesus taught his disciples perhaps the biggest lesson of all. Or, rather, he coalesced all his previous teaching in this one grand love feast and his actions during it. First, he makes an everlasting sacrament out of self-giving. We not only receive his risen Body and Blood for our nourishment, but we also challenge ourselves to participate in this same act of self-giving, this same act of love. To proclaim, we must participate. To participate, we must give ourselves over for others as did Jesus. Second, Jesus gave us a profound witness to what self-giving love looks like: he washed his disciples' feet. This act of humble service is our "model to follow." We wash the feet of others when we love with the same kind of unreserved love as Jesus showed us. When we look beyond our own suffering to the needs of others. When we look beyond misunderstanding and betrayal to persons who are broken and need forgiveness, who need to be loved into new life. This footwashing is more than a ritual act. It is a way of living and loving. This sums up all Jesus taught.

✦ I offer to others the self-giving, loving service Jesus modeled for me in these ways . . .

Brief Silence

Prayer

We raise grateful hearts to you, O God, for the wondrous gift of the risen Jesus' Body and Blood. May our reverence increase, our wonder and awe deepen, and our gratitude have no end. We ask this through Christ our Lord. **Amen.**

On Easter our Lenten penance gives way to the exuberant joy of celebrating Christ's resurrection. Let us resolve to witness by our lives to this new Life and ready ourselves to give God heartfelt thanks and praise during our prayer and reflection . . .

Prayer

Glorious God of the resurrection, your Son conquered death and opened for us the door to a share in his risen Life. May we be faithful witnesses to his continued Presence among us. By our witness may we instill deeper faith and sure hope in those we encounter in his Name. We ask this through Christ our Lord. **Amen.**

Gospel (John 20:1-9)

On the first day of the week, Mary of Magdala came to the tomb early in the morning, while it was still dark, and saw the stone removed from the tomb. So she ran and went to Simon Peter and to the other disciple whom Jesus loved, and told them, "They have taken the Lord from the tomb, and we don't know where they put him." So Peter and the other disciple went out and came to the tomb. They both ran, but the other disciple ran faster than Peter and arrived at the tomb first; he bent down and saw the burial cloths there, but did not go in. When Simon Peter arrived after him, he went into the tomb and saw the burial cloths there, and the cloth that had covered his head, not with the burial cloths but rolled up in a separate place. Then the other disciple also went in, the one who had arrived at the tomb first, and he saw and believed. For they did not yet understand the Scripture that he had to rise from the dead.

Brief Silence

For Reflection

The news of an empty tomb spread from Mary to Peter and the disciple. They ran—hope quickens us. They believed—faith urges us. They witnessed to the good news—good news cannot be contained. Good news such as an empty tomb and soon an encounter with the risen One not only cannot be contained, it changes us. Like Mary and the disciples we become witnesses to Christ's risen Life. Our encounters with the risen One compel us to be witnesses, to spread Easter joy. Perhaps this is why we are so awed at the mystery: not just that Jesus was raised from the dead, but that God entrusts us with continuing Jesus' saving mission and with being witnesses to God's mighty deed of resurrection. It appears as though God trusts us a great deal. This trust is like the baptismal waters washing us anew, strengthening us to proclaim the unbelievable—that the tomb is empty; the crucified One is raised from the dead. Our witnessing to his saving acts move us from our own comfort zones of life to radiating the joy of the risen One's dwelling within and among us.

✦ I have "told" others about Jesus' risen Life in which I share by . . .

Brief Silence

Prayer

God of joy and new Life, give us during this holy season of Easter a renewed commitment to live the Gospel as Jesus taught us, to witness to his Presence by our daily good works, and to grow in our love for the gift of his continued Presence in the Holy Eucharist. We ask this through Christ our Lord. **Amen.**

Thomas doubted that Jesus had risen from the dead and only came to believe when he saw the risen Jesus. During our prayer and reflection, may we encounter Christ and come to deeper belief in his risen Presence among us . . .

Prayer

God of peace and trust, your risen Son bestowed on the fearful disciples locked in the Upper Room the Holy Spirit who enabled them to rejoice in the new Life of the resurrection and Jesus' Presence among them. Take away from us any unrest or lack of trust we have, and give us the confidence to journey with him through death to fullness of Life. We ask this through Christ our Lord. **Amen.**

Gospel (John 20:19-31)

On the evening of that first day of the week, when the doors were locked, where the disciples were, for fear of the Jews, Jesus came and stood in their midst and said to them, "Peace be with you." When he had said this, he showed them his hands and his side. The disciples rejoiced when they saw the Lord. Jesus said to them again, "Peace be with you. As the Father has sent me, so I send you." And when he had said this, he breathed on them and said to them, "Receive the Holy Spirit. Whose sins you forgive are forgiven them, and whose sins you retain are retained."

Thomas, called Didymus, one of the Twelve, was not with them when Jesus came. So the other disciples said to him, "We have seen the Lord." But he said to them, "Unless I see the mark of the nails in his hands and put my finger into the nailmarks and put my hand into his side, I will not believe."

Now a week later his disciples were again inside and Thomas was with them. Jesus came, although the doors were locked, and stood in their midst and said, "Peace be with you." Then he said to Thomas, "Put your finger here and see my hands, and bring your hand and put it into my side, and do not be unbelieving, but believe." Thomas answered and said to him, "My Lord and my God!" Jesus said to him, "Have you come to believe because you have seen me? Blessed are those who have not seen and have believed."

Now, Jesus did many other signs in the presence of his disciples that are not written in this book. But these are written that you may come to believe that Jesus is the Christ, the Son of God, and that through this belief you may have life in his name.

Brief Silence

For Reflection

It's been only three days since the disciples have seen Jesus alive. But it must seem like an eternity to them. The disciples are gathered behind locked doors. They are afraid. They are confused about what to do. So they stay put. They are stuck. They've lost the sense of confidence they had when Jesus was with them. Probably their sense of peace has been shattered as well. On Easter evening, the risen Jesus appears and shows the disciples "his hands and his side." It is Jesus who makes the first, convincing move to enable the disciples to believe that he has truly risen from the dead. It is he who wants the disciples to see him, to regain their confidence and peace. To this end, he bestows upon them the gift of the Holy Spirit. With this gift, the disciples are able to rejoice, to believe that he is truly risen. The disciples have never before seen *this* Jesus. He bears the marks of suffering and death. Yet he is risen, never to die again. He has conquered death, for himself and for all of us.

✦ The way I express my belief in the risen Jesus in my daily living is carried over in how I distribute Holy Communion by . . .

Brief Silence

Prayer

What peace and joy, gracious God, our share in the Holy Eucharist brings us! May we rejoice at all you give us, share your gifts with others, and one day come to share eternally in the Life the risen Son gained for us. We ask this through Christ our Lord. **Amen.**

The risen Jesus appears to the disciples and calls them to witness both to his resurrection and to God's offer of forgiveness. May we deepen our commitment to be Jesus' faithful followers and witnesses . . .

Prayer

Faithful God, you forgive those who come to you with contrite hearts. But how hard it is sometimes for us to forgive one another! Help us to be a forgiving people, so that we might share in a new way in the joy of Jesus' risen Life. We ask this through Christ our Lord. **Amen.**

Gospel (Luke 24:35-48)

The two disciples recounted what had taken place on the way, and how Jesus was made known to them in the breaking of bread.

While they were still speaking about this, he stood in their midst and said to them, "Peace be with you." But they were startled and terrified and thought that they were seeing a ghost. Then he said to them, "Why are you troubled? And why do questions arise in your hearts? Look at my hands and my feet, that it is I myself. Touch me and see, because a ghost does not have flesh and bones as you can see I have." And as he said this, he showed them his hands and his feet. While they were still incredulous for joy and were amazed, he asked them, "Have you anything here to eat?" They gave him a piece of baked fish; he took it and ate it in front of them.

He said to them, "These are my words that I spoke to you while I was still with you, that everything written about me in the law of Moses and in the prophets and psalms must be fulfilled." Then he opened their minds to understand the Scriptures. And he said to them, "Thus it is written that the Christ would suffer and rise from the dead on the third day and that repentance, for the forgiveness of sins, would be preached in his name to all the nations, beginning from Jerusalem. You are witnesses of these things."

Brief Silence

For Reflection

Why think about sins and forgiveness during Easter time? Easter is a joyful time to celebrate new Life! We, unlike the disciples to whom Jesus appeared after the resurrection, cannot look at, touch, see with our own eyes this Jesus who was dead and now is risen to new Life. Yet Jesus gives us another, just as concrete, means as physical encounter with him to come to belief in the new Life of resurrection. Repentance and forgiveness are themselves encounters with the risen Jesus, an invitation to deeper belief, and an experience of our own coming to a share in Jesus' risen Life. Jesus opened the minds of the disciples to grasp two things written in the Scriptures: that he "would suffer and rise from the dead," and that "repentance, for the forgiveness of sins, would be preached in his name to all the nations." Our repentance—conversion of life—turns us to the God who forgives and who fills us with the new Life of the resurrection. Ultimately, this risen Life within us empowers a way of living that witnesses to God's forgiveness of our sinfulness.

✦ The Eucharist has inspired and nourished me to be repentant and forgiving by . . .

Brief Silence

Prayer

Forgiving God, in the Holy Eucharist you draw us closer to you and one another and bring us to a desire to repent of all that alienates us from you and others. May we be forgiving of ourselves and others, and in this gracious act become more like your Son who taught us to forgive seventy times seven. We ask this through Christ our Lord. **Amen.**

Let us pray that we be empowered to hear the voice of Jesus the Good Shepherd. Let us also pray that we may be good shepherds ourselves, helping each other come to the fullness of Life . . .

Prayer

Shepherd God, you speak to us in the depths of our hearts and guide us along right paths. May we attune ourselves to your guiding voice and live your holy will as witnesses that you alone are our Good Shepherd. We ask this through Christ our Lord. **Amen.**

Gospel (John 10:11-18)

Jesus said: "I am the good shepherd. A good shepherd lays down his life for the sheep. A hired man, who is not a shepherd and whose sheep are not his own, sees a wolf coming and leaves the sheep and runs away, and the wolf catches and scatters them. This is because he works for pay and has no concern for the sheep. I am the good shepherd, and I know mine and mine know me, just as the Father knows me and I know the Father; and I will lay down my life for the sheep. I have other sheep that do not belong to this fold. These also I must lead, and they will hear my voice, and there will be one flock, one shepherd. This is why the Father loves me, because I lay down my life in order to take it up again. No one takes it from me, but I lay it down on my own. I have power to lay it down, and power to take it up again. This command I have received from my Father."

Brief Silence

For Reflection

Jesus proclaims that "I am the good shepherd" and "I know mine and mine know me." To know Jesus is to be one with him, the Good Shepherd. This means that we are not only sheep who hear our Good Shepherd's voice and come to know him, but we also are to become good shepherds ourselves. Transformed from sheep to shepherd, we take up the life our Good Shepherd has laid down. The good shepherd is concerned about, cares for, and protects the sheep even to the point of laying down the shepherd's life. Jesus requires of us disciples the same mission—to also lay down our lives (this phrase occurs five times in the gospel). Shepherding, then, is serious and dangerous business! It means that we cannot run away from danger like the hired man, but we must meet danger head-on for the sake of God's beloved. Because of our baptism, we share in the new Life of Christ; our entry into this new Life is dying to ourselves—laying down our own lives. We are strengthened to lay down our lives for others when Jesus' voice is the guiding element in our daily living.

✦ When I say "Body [Blood] of Christ" to communicants, I am the voice of the Good Shepherd when . . .

Brief Silence

Prayer

Caring God, your Son is our Good Shepherd and leads us to a share in his risen Life. May our Holy Communion unite us more closely with him, so that we more willingly embrace laying down our own lives for the good of others. We ask this through Christ our Lord. **Amen.**

May we become branches grafted onto the vine who is Christ and may we renew our commitment to remain in Christ . . .

Prayer

Life-giving God, you choose us humble servants to bear for others the fruit of your Presence. Help us to remain in the risen Jesus and thus continue his saving mission, bearing the wondrous fruit of his redeeming love for others. We ask this through Christ our Lord. **Amen.**

Gospel (John 15:1-8)

Jesus said to his disciples: "I am the true vine, and my Father is the vine grower. He takes away every branch in me that does not bear fruit, and every one that does he prunes so that it bears more fruit. You are already pruned because of the word that I spoke to you. Remain in me, as I remain in you. Just as a branch cannot bear fruit on its own unless it remains on the vine, so neither can you unless you remain in me. I am the vine, you are the branches. Whoever remains in me and I in him will bear much fruit, because without me you can do nothing. Anyone who does not remain in me will be thrown out like a branch and wither; people will gather them and throw them into a fire and they will be burned. If you remain in me and my words remain in you, ask for whatever you want and it will be done for you. By this is my Father glorified, that you bear much fruit and become my disciples."

Brief Silence

For Reflection

The pruning of which Jesus speaks in this gospel is simply a means to an end. The end is the bearing of much fruit. To this end, Jesus' word has a twofold purpose. On the one hand, his word is prophetic and prunes whatever drains life out of his disciples. On the other, his word is the very sap of life that enables disciples to remain in him and bear fruit. The good fruit we bear when we remain in Jesus is witnessing to Gospel living, drawing others to the Life Jesus offers in the Holy Spirit, and glorifying the Father by the choices we make to live as Jesus taught us. True discipleship is about bearing this fruit. True discipleship, on the one hand, is very personal and at hand: we must remain in Jesus, grow in our relationship with him, and listen to his words and take them into our heart as a habit of living. On the other hand, true discipleship is very other-centered and broad: we must reach out to the whole world. The fruit we bear by remaining in Jesus is continuing his ministry of bringing salvation to all people. Oh, how sweet is this fruit!

✦ The fruit my discipleship has already borne is . . . New fruit that I sense is budding in me is . . .

Brief Silence

Prayer

Loving God, help us to be open to the pruning your Son does in us when we receive his Body and Blood and so are transformed more perfectly into living members of his Body. May this pruning bring us to a share in the fullness of Life you offer us. We ask this through Christ our Lord. **Amen.**

During our prayer and reflection, let us renew our commitment to love one another as Jesus loves us and come to complete joy in him . . .

Prayer

God of joy and love, the Easter mystery draws us into the risen Life of your divine Son and calls us to take up his way of living. May we be faithful as he was to your divine will and through our faithfulness come to love more deeply and have joy in abundance. We ask this through Christ our Lord. **Amen.**

Gospel (John 15:9-17)

Jesus said to his disciples: "As the Father loves me, so I also love you. Remain in my love. If you keep my commandments, you will remain in my love, just as I have kept my Father's commandments and remain in his love.

"I have told you this so that my joy may be in you and your joy might be complete. This is my commandment: love one another as I love you. No one has greater love than this, to lay down one's life for one's friends. You are my friends if you do what I command you. I no longer call you slaves, because a slave does not know what his master is doing. I have called you friends, because I have told you everything I have heard from my Father. It was not you who chose me, but I who chose you and appointed you to go and bear fruit that will remain, so that whatever you ask the Father in my name he may give you. This I command you: love one another."

Brief Silence

For Reflection

Immediately after Jesus expresses the desire that his joy become complete in us, he commands us to "love one another." What is his joy? The deep resonance of risen Life that arises from being faithful to the Father's will. What is the love he commands? Laying "down one's life." Joy and love are the Easter mystery made visible. Love always brings us to Good Friday, because then we gaze upon the Jesus who lays down his life. This Jesus calls us to lay down our own life, to give ourselves over to the kind of self-giving life that brings Life to others. Joy always proclaims Easter Sunday, that day when Life burst forth from death. We who remain in Jesus' love and welcome his joy in us embody the Easter mystery, make visible God's saving events, witness to bearing the fruit of the Father's gift of Life. Jesus' love for us is the model: he sacrificed his life, so must we; he overcame death, so must we overcome our own reluctance to die to self for the good of others. Our joy can be complete only when we love as Jesus did.

✦ As a sacrament of love, Holy Communion helps me lay down my life for the good of others in that . . .

Brief Silence

Prayer

Ever-faithful God, through receiving Holy Communion we share in your divine Son's Body and Blood, in his risen Life. May our love and joy at receiving this great gift overflow in laying down our own life for others. We ask this through Christ our Lord. **Amen.**

As we commemorate the risen Lord's ascension into heaven and his commissioning of the disciples to preach the Gospel, may our prayer and reflection bring us to become more perfectly Jesus' disciples who are commissioned and sent . . .

Prayer

Ever-living God, your divine Son commissions his disciples to proclaim the Gospel and continue his work of salvation. Strengthen us for this sacred task, that we might go forth armed with the Presence of the risen Son and with the courage to be bold and true to what he taught us. We ask this through Christ our Lord. **Amen.**

Gospel (Mark 16:15-20)

Jesus said to his disciples: "Go into the whole world and proclaim the gospel to every creature. Whoever believes and is baptized will be saved; whoever does not believe will be condemned. These signs will accompany those who believe: in my name they will drive out demons, they will speak new languages. They will pick up serpents with their hands, and if they drink any deadly thing, it will not harm them. They will lay hands on the sick, and they will recover."

So then the Lord Jesus, after he spoke to them, was taken up into heaven and took his seat at the right hand of God. But they went forth and preached everywhere, while the Lord worked with them and confirmed the word through accompanying signs.

Brief Silence

For Reflection

The ascension marks the completion of Jesus' historical ministry and the beginning of our own commission to proclaim the Gospel. We are not forced to proclaim the Gospel, nor do we do this on our own authority. We undertake our mission through the Holy Spirit and manifest the Holy Spirit through our mission. But always the mission is Christ's. At first this might seem an impossible commission, and surely on our own authority we cannot be faithful to it.

As the Jesus of history takes his leave of this world, it is clear that he intends his saving mission to continue. Seemingly without question, fear, or hesitation, the disciples "went forth." But they did not go forth alone: "the Lord worked with them." The mission, the work, and the signs are of the Lord Jesus. The disciples "who went forth and preached everywhere" were of the Lord Jesus. This relationship is the guarantee of Jesus' continued mission. So the gospel raises this question for disciples today: Are we of the Lord Jesus?

✦ My distribution of Holy Communion continues the mission of the Lord Jesus in that . . .

Brief Silence

Prayer

Through receiving the risen Jesus' Body and Blood, may we be nourished to go forth, knowing that we are never alone, for the risen Jesus is always with us. Strengthen our relationship with him so that we may be true to his Gospel and one day share the fullness of his risen Life. We ask this through Christ our Lord. **Amen.**

May this time of reflection strengthen us to speak Christ's word of truth to the world. Let us pray that we are faithful to this mission given to us . . .

Prayer

We are overwhelmed, loving God, by the risen Jesus' intimate prayer for us. Increase our love and joy, that our prayer for others might be so intimate and true. We ask this through Christ our Lord. **Amen.**

Gospel (John 17:11b-19)

Lifting up his eyes to heaven, Jesus prayed, saying: "Holy Father, keep them in your name that you have given me, so that they may be one just as we are one. When I was with them I protected them in your name that you gave me, and I guarded them, and none of them was lost except the son of destruction, in order that the Scripture might be fulfilled. But now I am coming to you. I speak this in the world so that they may share my joy completely. I gave them your word, and the world hated them, because they do not belong to the world any more than I belong to the world. I do not ask that you take them out of the world but that you keep them from the evil one. They do not belong to the world any more than I belong to the world. Consecrate them in the truth. Your word is truth. As you sent me into the world, so I sent them into the world. And I consecrate myself for them, so that they also may be consecrated in truth."

Brief Silence

For Reflection

Jesus' prayer for his disciples at the Last Supper is very self-revealing. We can feel his anguish, love, and concern. Jesus trusts that his disciples will take up his mission, and knows full well that we will face the same fate as he is facing—death. No wonder his prayer is so intense and personal! Jesus is not naive about sending out disciples. His lengthy prayer for them (and us) recognizes that there will be resistance ("the world hated them") to the word of truth. Nevertheless, Jesus' prayer assures us that we are never alone. We are one with each other in the Body of Christ. In spite of the hard work of proclaiming the Gospel and meeting resistance, disciples experience joy because their relationship with God is secure. Such confidence Jesus spawns in us by his prayer! This is our joy: to be so intimately loved, cared for, protected, guarded, and guided by Jesus—all for the sake of the world. Our relationship with God is secure because Jesus prays for us, makes us one with him, and promises that we will remain in him because of his gift of the Holy Spirit.

✦ Some of the resistance I've met in being faithful to Jesus' mission is . . . Who/what has helped me overcome this resistance is . . .

Brief Silence

Prayer

Holy Communion, dear God, helps us to face the resistance of living the Gospel. May this nourishment banish our anguish and discouragement and increase in us the love and joy that union with you brings. We ask this through Christ our Lord. **Amen.**

May our reflection be for us a reminder of the gift of the Spirit given us at baptism. Let us pray to live faithfully the life to which the Spirit calls us . . .

Prayer

God of Spirit and truth, our fidelity and proclamation of the Gospel by the way we live brings you glory. Increase our faithfulness and boldness in proclaiming the Good News your Son taught us. We ask this through Christ our Lord. **Amen.**

Gospel (John 15:26-27; 16:12-15)

Jesus said to his disciples: "When the Advocate comes whom I will send you from the Father, the Spirit of truth that proceeds from the Father, he will testify to me. And you also testify, because you have been with me from the beginning.

"I have much more to tell you, but you cannot bear it now. But when he comes, the Spirit of truth, he will guide you to all truth. He will not speak on his own, but he will speak what he hears, and will declare to you the things that are coming. He will glorify me, because he will take from what is mine and declare it to you. Everything that the Father has is mine; for this reason I told you that he will take from what is mine and declare it to you."

Brief Silence

For Reflection

According to this gospel, both the Spirit and the disciples testify to Jesus. What is this testimony? It is the revelation that Jesus is of the Father, is the divine Son. Furthermore, this gospel says that the Spirit glorifies Jesus by testifying. So then do we. What is this glory? It is Jesus himself who is the visible Presence of the Father. Like the Spirit of truth, when we testify we also glorify.

This Pentecost commemoration does not simply recall a past event, but celebrates what God is doing within us now. In baptism each of us received the Spirit; that is our Pentecost. The Spirit is not something we have, is not a possession. The Spirit dwells within us as divine Life, enabling us to be faithful and true disciples. The Spirit is given for the sake of mission: to proclaim the gospel ("you also testify"), to be molded as disciples ("the Spirit . . . will guide you to all truth"), and, ultimately, to worship ("glorify me"). The indwelling of the Spirit is a continual Pentecost so that everyone may bring glory to God.

✦ Every time I distribute Holy Communion, I celebrate Pentecost in that . . .

Brief Silence

Prayer

Triune God, Father, Son, and Holy Spirit, you dwell within us and your divine Presence enables us to testify to the Good News the divine Son taught us. May we live our lives as a continual Pentecost and always bring you glory. We ask this through Christ our Lord. **Amen.**

We honor the Most Holy Trinity in whose name we have been baptized. Let us prepare for our time of prayer and reflection by calling to mind the times we have not been faithful to our baptismal commitment . . .

Prayer

Wondrous God, you reveal to us the intimacy of your divine Being: three Persons united in one God through love. Knowing we are baptized in the triune Name, help us to raise our hearts in gratitude for the great gift of your divine Presence dwelling within us. We ask this through Christ our Lord. **Amen.**

Gospel (Matt 28:16-20)

The eleven disciples went to Galilee, to the mountain to which Jesus had ordered them. When they all saw him, they worshiped, but they doubted. Then Jesus approached and said to them, "All power in heaven and on earth has been given to me. Go, therefore, and make disciples of all nations, baptizing them in the name of the Father, and of the Son, and of the Holy Spirit, teaching them to observe all that I have commanded you. And behold, I am with you always, until the end of the age."

Brief Silence

For Reflection

In this gospel passage for the solemnity of the Most Holy Trinity, Jesus commands the disciples to baptize "in the name of the Father, and of the Son, and of the Holy Spirit." Jesus reveals his undivided, divine relationship with the Father when he declares, "All power in heaven and on earth has been given to me." Baptism professes our faith in the Holy Trinity and celebrates our insertion into the intimate, relational life of Father, Son, and Holy Spirit. To share in divine identity is to share in divine doing—we, too, are to do mighty deeds. To be formed into the identity of Christ is to be formed into his mission. The gospel rather succinctly and clearly lays out the mission with which Jesus charged the disciples (and us) before he ascended into heaven: make disciples, baptize in the name of the Trinity, teach, and observe "all that [Jesus] has commanded." Jesus can entrust this mission to us because we share in his identity through the power of the Spirit. This identity is the fruit of our fidelity. Has anything more wondrous or greater happened before?

✦ The Trinity influences how I relate to others by . . . This affects my ministry in that . . .

Brief Silence

Prayer

Through the mystery of baptism and the Holy Eucharist, O triune God, we share in the mystery of your divine majesty. May we live this mystery to the fullest and one day come to be one with you for ever and ever. We ask this through Christ our Lord. **Amen.**

With this solemnity, we celebrate Jesus' gift to us of his Body and Blood for our strength and nourishment. Let us prepare for our prayer and reflection by asking God's mercy for the times we have not lived up to the promise of this gift . . .

Prayer

You call a holy people to yourself, O God, and in the gift of your Son's Body and Blood we are nourished to remain your holy people. May we grow in our gratitude for the Holy Eucharist, sustain others by our self-giving, and commit ourselves more deeply to eucharistic living. We ask this through Christ our Lord. **Amen.**

Gospel (Mark 14:12-16, 22-26)

On the first day of the Feast of Unleavened Bread, when they sacrificed the Passover lamb, Jesus' disciples said to him, "Where do you want us to go and prepare for you to eat the Passover?" He sent two of his disciples and said to them, "Go into the city and a man will meet you, carrying a jar of water. Follow him. Wherever he enters, say to the master of the house, 'The Teacher says, "Where is my guest room where I may eat the Passover with my disciples?"' Then he will show you a large upper room furnished and ready. Make the preparations for us there." The disciples then went off, entered the city, and found it just as he had told them; and they prepared the Passover.

While they were eating, he took bread, said the blessing, broke it, gave it to them, and said, "Take it; this is my body." Then he took a cup, gave thanks, and gave it to them, and they all drank from it. He said to them, "This is my blood of the covenant, which will be shed for many. Amen, I say to you, I shall not drink again the fruit of the vine until the day when I drink it new in the kingdom of God." Then, after singing a hymn, they went out to the Mount of Olives.

Brief Silence

For Reflection

Jesus wants to "eat the Passover with [his] disciples." This annual festival celebrates the Jewish people "passing over" from lives of slavery and drudgery in Egypt to lives of freedom and abundance in the Promised Land. This meal portends another passover— Jesus' own passing over from suffering and death to risen Life. Through our baptism we enter into Jesus' mystery of dying and rising. And yet another passover: our passing over from old self to new self, from life of sin to life of grace. Each Eucharist, each time we eat and drink the Body and Blood of Christ, we embrace anew our passing over to new Life in Christ.

Each celebration of the Eucharist is a passover for us. It celebrates our plunging ever more deeply into the paschal mystery, into Jesus' passing from death to risen Life. It celebrates our embrace of the new identity baptism first bestows on us and Eucharist celebrates and nourishes: that we ourselves are members of the Body of Christ. As Jesus continually gives himself to us in the mystery of his Body and Blood, so does Eucharist call us to the same self-giving.

✦ My distributing the Body and Blood of Christ is carried forth in a self-giving way of living when I . . .

Brief Silence

Prayer

Each time we celebrate the Eucharist, gracious God, we pass over to a richer membership in the Body of Christ. May Jesus' gift of self spur us on to our own greater self-giving and bring us to fullness of Life with you. We ask this through Christ our Lord. **Amen.**

The kingdom of God grows and bears fruit when we hear God's word and nurture it in our hearts. As we begin our time of prayer and reflection, we pause to seek God's mercy for the times we have not listened to God's word and responded in our lives . . .

Prayer

Your kingdom, O God, is your reign among us. Strengthen us to do your holy will, to live the Gospel, and to be living parables of your gift of Life and holiness to us. We ask this through Christ our Lord. **Amen.**

Gospel (Mark 4:26-34)

Jesus said to the crowds: "This is how it is with the kingdom of God; it is as if a man were to scatter seed on the land and would sleep and rise night and day and through it all the seed would sprout and grow, he knows not how. Of its own accord the land yields fruit, first the blade, then the ear, then the full grain in the ear. And when the grain is ripe, he wields the sickle at once, for the harvest has come."

He said, "To what shall we compare the kingdom of God, or what parable can we use for it? It is like a mustard seed that, when it is sown in the ground, is the smallest of all the seeds on the earth. But once it is sown, it springs up and becomes the largest of plants and puts forth large branches, so that the birds of the sky can dwell in its shade." With many such parables he spoke the word to them as they were able to understand it. Without parables he did not speak to them, but to his own disciples he explained everything in private.

Brief Silence

For Reflection

In this gospel both the land and the mustard seed actualize their potential—they do what by nature they are created to do. These two parables are used by Jesus to help us grasp what is surely a mystery: the "kingdom of God." This kingdom is not a place or space. It is not something we can discover or conquer. Instead, these parables invite us to be who we are and allow God's kingdom to conquer us. These parables call us to surrender to God's word and action within us, to cooperate with God in bringing about a world filled with abundance and promise. These parables challenge us to make the kingdom of God a visible reality shaping our daily living. The "kingdom of God" is visible when we, like the land and mustard seed, actualize our own potential and do what we are called to do as Jesus' disciples. In this way we become living parables doing what God created us to do and being who God created us to be. In the end we ourselves are God's abundant harvest. And perhaps this is the greatest mystery of all.

✦ I make the kingdom of God visible in my ministry when I . . . in my daily living when I . . .

Brief Silence

Prayer

Gracious God, through Holy Communion we are strengthened to reach the full stature you call us to as members of the Body of Christ. May this nourishment fill us with your Life and love, helping us more faithfully to reach out to others. We ask this through Christ our Lord. **Amen.**

In this gospel Jesus calms the storm at sea and leads the disciples to greater faith in who he is. Let us open ourselves to Jesus revealing himself and his saving power to us during our prayer and reflection . . .

Prayer

Almighty God, your Son came to us as One like us in all things but sin. Help us to grow in our relationship with him so that we might also come to know him more deeply as our Savior and Lord. We ask this through Christ our Lord. **Amen.**

Gospel (Mark 4:35-41)

On that day, as evening drew on, Jesus said to his disciples: "Let us cross to the other side." Leaving the crowd, they took Jesus with them in the boat just as he was. And other boats were with him. A violent squall came up and waves were breaking over the boat, so that it was already filling up. Jesus was in the stern, asleep on a cushion. They woke him and said to him, "Teacher, do you not care that we are perishing?" He woke up, rebuked the wind, and said to the sea, "Quiet! Be still!" The wind ceased and there was great calm. Then he asked them, "Why are you terrified? Do you not yet have faith?" They were filled with great awe and said to one another, "Who then is this whom even wind and sea obey?"

Brief Silence

For Reflection

At the end of a day of preaching and healing, Jesus was no doubt tired. The disciples took him in the boat "just as he was." So, Jesus fell fast asleep. When a "violent squall" arose, the disciples thought that Jesus didn't care that they were "perishing." But Jesus did care; he came precisely to save humanity from perishing. The boat was filling up with water from the waves, while the disciples' hearts were empty of the depth of faith needed to be calm, to be still, to know that Jesus surely does care for them. The disciples' faith is weak because the disciples do not yet know who Jesus is and why he came. When Jesus asked faith of the disciples, he was asking them to grow in their relationship to him as more than a "Teacher." He was revealing further that he was the long-expected Messiah, the Son of God. We have an advantage over the disciples in that boat on a stormy sea: we know who Jesus is. But nevertheless we must still ask the critical question: how strong is *our* faith?

✦ Distributing Holy Communion deepens my understanding of who Jesus is and why he came when I . . .

Brief Silence

Prayer

God of Life, your Presence dispels our fatigue, calms the violent storms within us, and keeps us from perishing. May the peace we receive from your sacrament of the Eucharist strengthen us to grow in our relationship with you and to come to know your divine Son more intimately. We ask this through Christ our Lord. **Amen.**

In this Sunday's gospel, because of their faith Jesus heals a woman and raises Jairus's daughter from the dead. Let us ask for God's mercy for those times when we failed to act on our faith . . .

Prayer

God of healing, we come to you with open hearts, with courage and expectation. Heal us of all illness, of whatever alienates us from you, of our own weakness and self-will. We ask this through Christ our Lord. **Amen.**

Gospel (Mark 5:21-24, 35b-43)

When Jesus had crossed again in the boat to the other side, a large crowd gathered around him, and he stayed close to the sea. One of the synagogue officials, named Jairus, came forward. Seeing him he fell at his feet and pleaded earnestly with him, saying, "My daughter is at the point of death. Please, come lay your hands on her that she may get well and live." He went off with him, and a large crowd followed him and pressed upon him.

While he was still speaking, people from the synagogue official's house arrived and said, "Your daughter has died; why trouble the teacher any longer?" Disregarding the message that was reported, Jesus said to the synagogue official, "Do not be afraid; just have faith." He did not allow anyone to accompany him inside except Peter, James, and John, the brother of James. When they arrived at the house of the synagogue official, he caught sight of a commotion, people weeping and wailing loudly. So he went in and said to them, "Why this commotion and weeping? The child is not dead but asleep." And they ridiculed him. Then he put them all out. He took along the child's father and mother and those who were with him and entered the room where the child was. He took the child by the hand and said to her, *"Talitha koum,"* which means, "Little girl, I say to you, arise!" The girl, a child of twelve, arose immediately and walked around. At that they were utterly astounded. He gave strict orders that no one should know this and said that she should be given something to eat.

Brief Silence

For Reflection

Faith in who Jesus is and what he can do brings us to act. Jairus approaches Jesus directly, kneels before him, and asks for healing for his daughter. The "woman afflicted with hemorrhages" dares not approach Jesus directly; she simply wishes to "touch his clothes" to be cured. In both cases their faith gave them the courage to approach Jesus and raised their expectation that he had the power to heal. Our faith, too, gives us courage and expectation. What do we do with it? Our first challenge is to come to Jesus with open hearts.

The faith of Jairus and the woman stand in opposition to the hardheaded realism of the disciples and the crowd. Coming to Jesus and encountering him always changes experience, situations, expectations. It is precisely Jairus's and the woman's faith that a new situation with a different outcome would be ushered in by the presence of Jesus that opened the door to the new Life Jesus offered. These humble petitioners make visible the faith to which the disciples, the crowd, and we are called. They teach us that faith is an act of seeking Jesus.

✦ When I see the communicants as those who want healing and new Life from Jesus, my ministry becomes . . .

Brief Silence

Prayer

Saving God, help us to reach out to touch your Presence in all the ways you come to us. May our faith grow deeper as we encounter you in the most unexpected ways. May our encounters bring us to an eternity of Life with you. We ask this through Christ our Lord. **Amen.**

This gospel describes the rejection of Jesus by those most familiar with him—his kin and neighbors. Let us ask God's mercy for the times we have rejected Jesus by our sinfulness . . .

Prayer

Faithful God, increase our weak faith. Help us to see who Jesus really is, to recognize his Presence among us, and to be open to the mighty deeds he works among those who do not reject him. We ask this through Christ our Lord. **Amen.**

Gospel (Mark 6:1-6)

Jesus departed from there and came to his native place, accompanied by his disciples. When the sabbath came he began to teach in the synagogue, and many who heard him were astonished. They said, "Where did this man get all this? What kind of wisdom has been given him? What mighty deeds are wrought by his hands! Is he not the carpenter, the son of Mary, and the brother of James and Joses and Judas and Simon? And are not his sisters here with us?" And they took offense at him. Jesus said to them, "A prophet is not without honor except in his native place and among his own kin and in his own house." So he was not able to perform any mighty deed there, apart from curing a few sick people by laying his hands on them. He was amazed at their lack of faith.

Brief Silence

For Reflection

The limited expectations of those in Jesus' "native place" blocked their ability to see in faith who Jesus really was. In response to Jesus' teaching and wisdom, mighty deeds and healings, "they took offense." Their limited expectations limited Jesus' own ability to show that a new in-breaking of God was among them. This gospel challenges us to examine the limits of our own expectations about who Jesus is and what he can do for us. Jesus is unable to work miracles for those who do not believe in him. The shock of the gospel is the weight that our faith or lack of faith has. God never pushes salvation on us; it is a faithful gift, but one freely given and only asking of us a free response. Jesus "was not able" to perform miracles in his hometown because of the townspeople's lack of faith. Shockingly, God never quits on us or abandons us; it is we who choose to resist or have faith. It is we who choose . . . is Jesus able to perform any mighty deed or not?

✦ My distributing Holy Communion challenges me to recognize Jesus among my "own kin" and "in [my] own house" because . . .

Brief Silence

Prayer

Loving God, through our receiving Holy Communion help us to expand our limited expectations of what Jesus is accomplishing in and through us. May our faith in him deepen through the Eucharist and one day may we share the fullness of Life with him. We ask this through Christ our Lord. **Amen.**

Jesus summons the Twelve to go out on the urgent mission of preaching repentance. Let us consider the times we have not heeded Jesus' summons to continue his mission in our own lives and ask for his mercy . . .

Prayer

O God who calls, forgives, and saves, strengthen us to respond to your invitation to take up Jesus' saving mission to bring repentance and healing to the world. May we be strong by preaching through the way we live, the way we forgive others, the way we overcome barriers and chasms that divide. We ask this through Christ our Lord. **Amen.**

Gospel (Mark 6:7-13)

Jesus summoned the Twelve and began to send them out two by two and gave them authority over unclean spirits. He instructed them to take nothing for the journey but a walking stick—no food, no sack, no money in their belts. They were, however, to wear sandals but not a second tunic. He said to them, "Wherever you enter a house, stay there until you leave. Whatever place does not welcome you or listen to you, leave there and shake the dust off your feet in testimony against them." So they went off and preached repentance. The Twelve drove out many demons, and they anointed with oil many who were sick and cured them.

Brief Silence

For Reflection

"Jesus *summoned* the Twelve." "Summoned" is a significant word here. This is a call that cannot be ignored because the mission is so urgent: to preach repentance. The mission is so urgent that the Twelve are not even to burden themselves with seeming necessities of life. The mission is so urgent that the Twelve are not even to stay with those who do not receive them or listen to them. The mission is so urgent that the Twelve are given Jesus' own authority to expel demons and cure illnesses. Jesus sends the Twelve off to preach repentance. The mission is so urgent because what is at stake is our relationship with God and each other. Repentance heals the wounds that separate; repentance overflows into forgiveness; repentance changes our behavior; repentance is basic to growth in our covenantal fidelity; repentance makes us whole again. It is an awesome thought that Jesus entrusts his mission to us. We cannot ignore Jesus' command performance to preach repentance. The mission of Jesus is so urgent that he must use others to reach out to all people at all times to bring them salvation. The mission is so urgent that . . .

✦ My ministry of distributing the Body (Blood) of the risen Jesus summons me to . . .

Brief Silence

Prayer

God of love, you strengthen us for the urgent mission to preach repentance and healing to all people. May our words be backed by generous deeds, our preaching be backed by Gospel living, the urgency of the mission prompt us to hear Jesus' summons to follow in his steps. We ask this through Christ our Lord. **Amen.**

Jesus is the caring Shepherd who teaches us and gives us rest. Let us reflect on the times we have not responded to Jesus and pray for his mercy . . .

Prayer

Loving God, you shepherd us when we are busy at work and when we are at life-renewing rest. Help us to discern others' needs and respond to them with the care with which you respond to us. We ask this through Christ our Lord. **Amen.**

Gospel (Mark 6:30-34)

The apostles gathered together with Jesus and reported all they had done and taught. He said to them, "Come away by yourselves to a deserted place and rest a while." People were coming and going in great numbers, and they had no opportunity even to eat. So they went off in the boat by themselves to a deserted place. People saw them leaving and many came to know about it. They hastened there on foot from all the towns and arrived at the place before them.

When he disembarked and saw the vast crowd, his heart was moved with pity for them, for they were like sheep without a shepherd; and he began to teach them many things.

Brief Silence

For Reflection

Jesus discerned the differing needs of the weary disciples and the persistent crowd, and responded to each accordingly. Jesus interrupted his rest to tend to their needs. He shepherded them beyond their need for healing to teach them what they needed to learn about the saving mission he came to fulfill. Jesus, the true shepherd of God, always responds to the needs of others. How does Jesus respond when the apostles return from their mission and report to him? He invites them to come away and rest. How does Jesus respond when the crowd persists in hastening to him? He teaches them. In fact, he shepherds both the apostles and the crowd. Jesus shepherds everyone toward fuller life through both the re-creating power of rest and the transforming possibilities of new teaching. Jesus is ever the caring shepherd. Jesus is the divine shepherd who both knows the needs of others and responds to them. Jesus never misleads. By his own good example, Jesus teaches that responding to others' needs, fostering caring relationships, and teaching the Good News are at the heart of bringing his mission to completion.

✦ I experience my ministry of distributing Holy Communion as responding to communicants' needs in that . . .

Brief Silence

Prayer

Ever-living God, you invite us to come away and rest as we celebrate the Holy Eucharist. Help us always to hasten to you, to be taught by you, and to be guided by you, the shepherd God who desires that one day we enjoy the fullness of Life with you forever. We ask this through Christ our Lord. **Amen.**

Jesus feeds the five thousand with a few loaves and fishes. Let us ask for God's mercy for the times we have not been grateful for the abundance of God's gifts to us . . .

Prayer

God of generous abundance, you give to us even when we do not know how to ask, you feed us even when we do not know we are hungry for you, you bring us to fulfillment even when we do not know that we are lacking. May we be ever grateful for your care of us. We ask this through Christ our Lord. **Amen.**

Gospel (John 6:1-15)

Jesus went across the Sea of Galilee. A large crowd followed him, because they saw the signs he was performing on the sick. Jesus went up on the mountain, and there he sat down with his disciples. The Jewish feast of Passover was near. When Jesus raised his eyes and saw that a large crowd was coming to him, he said to Philip, "Where can we buy enough food for them to eat?" He said this to test him, because he himself knew what he was going to do. Philip answered him, "Two hundred days' wages worth of food would not be enough for each of them to have a little." One of his disciples, Andrew, the brother of Simon Peter, said to him, "There is a boy here who has five barley loaves and two fish; but what good are these for so many?" Jesus said, "Have the people recline." Now there was a great deal of grass in that place. So the men reclined, about five thousand in number. Then Jesus took the loaves, gave thanks, and distributed them to those who were reclining, and also as much of the fish as they wanted. When they had had their fill, he said to his disciples, "Gather the fragments left over, so that nothing will be wasted." So they collected them, and filled twelve wicker baskets with fragments from the five barley loaves that had been more than they could eat. When the people saw the sign he had done, they said, "This is truly the Prophet, the one who is to come into the world." Since Jesus knew that they were going to come and carry him off to make him king, he withdrew again to the mountain alone.

Brief Silence

For Reflection

Let's let a miracle be a miracle! Jesus tested Philip, who failed the test because he fixated on calculating the amount of food needed to feed the hungry crowd and its cost. He couldn't even imagine another way. Jesus, however, "knew what he was going to do"—he gave the crowd "as much . . . as they wanted." Amazingly, the miracle of giving them "as much . . . as they wanted" was still less than the other miracle Jesus gave them: "the sign" of the fullness of messianic Life. So much Life—even "twelve wicker baskets" more than they wanted.

The abundance in this multiplication account points to an eschatological sign of risen Life, a time of fulfillment when God's plan for redemption is finally realized. Even the context of this gospel passage points to a time of fulfillment: it is Passover—Israel's annual celebration of God's mighty deeds on their behalf. The wondrous and impressive sign that Jesus works on this occasion—feeding five thousand with five loaves—points beyond taking care of the hunger of the "large crowd." Rather, Jesus' sign points to a time when God's mighty deeds come to fulfillment—a time when all people are abundantly filled and every need is met.

✦ I become most aware of Holy Communion being "the sign" of the fullness of messianic Life when . . .

Brief Silence

Prayer

Gracious God, you give us more than we could ever want in the gift of your Son's Body and Blood. May we always receive this gift with reverence and awe, and one day come to the fullness of Life with you. We ask this through Christ our Lord. **Amen.**

Jesus is the Bread of Life, given to us as our everlasting Food. We pray to come to a deeper relationship with Jesus and ask forgiveness for the times we have not responded to his gift of himself . . .

Prayer

O God, you feed us with the gift of the finest wheat and the sweetness of the finest grape. May we seek only the food and drink that leads us to eternal Life. We ask this through Christ our Lord. **Amen.**

Gospel (John 6:24-35)

When the crowd saw that neither Jesus nor his disciples were there, they themselves got into boats and came to Capernaum looking for Jesus. And when they found him across the sea they said to him, "Rabbi, when did you get here?" Jesus answered them and said, "Amen, amen, I say to you, you are looking for me not because you saw signs but because you ate the loaves and were filled. Do not work for food that perishes but for the food that endures for eternal life, which the Son of Man will give you. For on him the Father, God, has set his seal." So they said to him, "What can we do to accomplish the works of God?" Jesus answered and said to them, "This is the work of God, that you believe in the one he sent." So they said to him, "What sign can you do, that we may see and believe in you? What can you do? Our ancestors ate manna in the desert, as it is written: / *He gave them bread from heaven to eat.*" / So Jesus said to them, "Amen, amen, I say to you, it was not Moses who gave the bread from heaven; my Father gives you the true bread from heaven. For the bread of God is that which comes down from heaven and gives life to the world."

So they said to him, "Sir, give us this bread always." Jesus said to them, "I am the bread of life; whoever comes to me will never hunger, and whoever believes in me will never thirst."

Brief Silence

For Reflection

What the crowd was not prepared for was that the bread Jesus offers is so much more than food that satisfies their immediate hunger. The bread the crowd seeks is perishable. They eat this bread but become hungry again—they must keep procuring this bread. The bread Jesus offers is eternal. Those who eat this bread will never hunger again. They cannot procure this bread because it is the Father's gift: the "true bread from heaven" that is Jesus himself. There is a tension—a grave misunderstanding—between what the crowd seeks and what Jesus offers. What do we seek?

Do we seek only nourishment? Or do we seek the Bread only God can give—Bread that is abundant and Life-giving? God's abundance is a sign of messianic times, of God's reign being established, of eternal Life. Our sharing in this abundance is already a sharing in the fullness of Life to come. The "bread of God . . . which comes down from heaven . . . gives life to the world." We consume the bread from heaven so that the mystery of Life may consume us, drawing us to eternal Life.

✦ Distributing the Bread of Life to the community nourishes my own daily living by . . .

Brief Silence

Prayer

We can never have enough, good God, of the bread from heaven that is no less than the true Body and Blood of your risen Son. May we enter into this mystery with eagerness to be filled with your very Life, the Life that leads us to an everlasting share in the risen Son's glory. We ask this through Christ our Lord. **Amen.**

God desires eternal Life for us and sends the Son as Bread from heaven to nourish and strengthen us. Let us prepare ourselves for our time of prayer and reflection by thanking God for this great gift . . .

Prayer

Ever-living God, you reveal to us through your divine Son the mystery of the Life you offer us through him. As we ponder the risen Jesus as the Bread of Life, may we come to a greater desire to share more often in such a great mystery. We ask this through Christ our Lord. **Amen.**

Gospel (John 6:41-51)

The Jews murmured about Jesus because he said, "I am the bread that came down from heaven," and they said, "Is this not Jesus, the son of Joseph? Do we not know his father and mother? Then how can he say, 'I have come down from heaven'?" Jesus answered and said to them, "Stop murmuring among yourselves. No one can come to me unless the Father who sent me draw him, and I will raise him on the last day. It is written in the prophets: / *They shall all be taught by God.* / Everyone who listens to my Father and learns from him comes to me. Not that anyone has seen the Father except the one who is from God; he has seen the Father. Amen, amen, I say to you, whoever believes has eternal life. I am the bread of life. Your ancestors ate the manna in the desert, but they died; this is the bread that comes down from heaven so that one may eat it and not die. I am the living bread that came down from heaven; whoever eats this bread will live forever; and the bread that I will give is my flesh for the life of the world."

Brief Silence

For Reflection

"The Jews murmured" because they could not get beyond their limited perception of who they thought Jesus was to the mystery about himself he reveals: "I am the bread of life," the Bread "come down from heaven," the Bread to whom we must come, the Bread who gives us a share in his "eternal life," the Bread in whom we must believe, the Bread who gives Self "for the life of the world." Jesus persists in revealing himself as the Bread sent by God to nourish the crowd (and us) for the journey to eternal Life. Jesus gives his life so that we might have new Life: "the bread that I will give is my flesh for the life of the world." The surprise of the gospel is that Jesus himself, as the "bread . . . from heaven," is both the promise and fulfillment of the eternal Life for which we long. Jesus declares himself to be "the living bread" and when we share in this Bread we "will live forever." Such mystery! Who can believe it? Who can afford not to believe it?

✦ When I come to Jesus, "the bread of life," what happens is . . .

Brief Silence

Prayer

Our Holy Communion, dear God, is the Bread of Life, the gift of your Son's very self, the wonder of the promise of eternal Life. As we receive this Body and Blood, may we long for the day of final fulfillment, when you give us an eternal share in your Life. We ask this through Christ our Lord. **Amen.**

ASSUMPTION OF THE BLESSED VIRGIN MARY

Mary was taken into heaven body and soul to enjoy eternal Life with her divine Son. Let us ask for God's mercy for the times when we have not been faithful as Mary was faithful . . .

Prayer

God of salvation, you kept Mary free from sin from the moment of her conception, and brought her home to you in both body and soul. May we imitate Mary's faithfulness in our own lives, always saying yes to your divine will. We ask this through Christ our Lord. **Amen.**

Gospel **(Luke 1:39-56; At the Mass during the Day)**

Mary set out and traveled to the hill country in haste to a town of Judah, where she entered the house of Zechariah and greeted Elizabeth. When Elizabeth heard Mary's greeting, the infant leaped in her womb, and Elizabeth, filled with the Holy Spirit, cried out in a loud voice and said, "Blessed are you among women, and blessed is the fruit of your womb. And how does this happen to me, that the mother of my Lord should come to me? For at the moment the sound of your greeting reached my ears, the infant in my womb leaped for joy. Blessed are you who believed that what was spoken to you by the Lord would be fulfilled."

And Mary said: / "My soul proclaims the greatness of the Lord; / my spirit rejoices in God my Savior / for he has looked with favor on his lowly servant. / From this day all generations will call me blessed: / the Almighty has done great things for me / and holy is his Name. / He has mercy on those who fear him / in every generation. / He has shown the strength of his arm, / and has scattered the proud in their conceit. / He has cast down the mighty from their thrones, / and has lifted up the lowly. / He has filled the hungry with good things, / and the rich he has sent away empty. / He has come to the help of his servant Israel / for he has remembered his promise of mercy, / the promise he made to our fathers, / to Abraham and his children forever."

Mary remained with her about three months and then returned to her home.

Brief Silence

For Reflection

Journeys that we plan have a beginning and an end. We leave, reach our destination, do what we journeyed to do, then return home. Journeys we plan are like circles—we come back home from where we began. This gospel's context is a planned journey. "Mary set out." However, her journey extended far beyond traveling to Elizabeth to help her in her need. Its duration was actually Mary's lifelong journey of praising God, of allowing God to do great things through her, of showing how God is turning upside down the order of things, of being an instrument for God to keep the divine promise of salvation.

This day we celebrate the completion of Mary's journey, when she "returned to her home," being taken body and soul into heaven to be forever with her Lord whom she bore in her womb. Mary's journey comes full circle—she began life united with God for she was conceived without sin, in perfect holiness. She concludes life by being united with God. When our life journey parallels Mary's journey of fidelity, then we, too, come "home."

✦ My life journey is calling me to set out to . . . for . . .

Brief Silence

Prayer

God of Life and holiness, you brought Mary body and soul to her true home in you. Bring us home, too, to enjoy with Mary and all the saints an eternity of offering you praise and thanksgiving. We ask this through Christ our Lord. **Amen.**

Jesus invites us in this gospel to eat his Body and drink his Blood that we may have Life. Let us prepare ourselves through our prayer and reflection to participate more consciously in this great mystery . . .

Prayer

God of Life, your divine Son gives himself to us as the Bread of Life. As we share in this great mystery, help us to come to know the risen Jesus better and to live as he taught us, bringing the Good News of salvation to all we meet. We ask this through Christ our Lord. **Amen.**

Gospel (John 6:51-58)

Jesus said to the crowds: "I am the living bread that came down from heaven; whoever eats this bread will live forever; and the bread that I will give is my flesh for the life of the world."

The Jews quarreled among themselves, saying, "How can this man give us his flesh to eat?" Jesus said to them, "Amen, amen, I say to you, unless you eat the flesh of the Son of Man and drink his blood, you do not have life within you. Whoever eats my flesh and drinks my blood has eternal life, and I will raise him on the last day. For my flesh is true food, and my blood is true drink. Whoever eats my flesh and drinks my blood remains in me and I in him. Just as the living Father sent me and I have life because of the Father, so also the one who feeds on me will have life because of me. This is the bread that came down from heaven. Unlike your ancestors who ate and still died, whoever eats this bread will live forever."

Brief Silence

For Reflection

Who is "this man"? This question underlies the quarrel the Jews in this gospel are having "among themselves." Jesus declares that he is "living bread" sent by his "living Father"; he shares divine Life with the Father. In Jesus divine Life has been incarnated in human flesh. When we eat his flesh and drink his blood, we partake in this same divine Life. And so, like God, we will "live forever." And so, like the risen Christ, we will be the Presence of God incarnated in human flesh. What a mystery! Its depth challenges us no less than the Jews of Jesus' time. We, too, are faced with the question, Who is "this man"?

We spend our lives encountering Jesus in many different ways and grappling with the mystery of who he is and what he did for us. The mystery of life and death is at the heart of Eucharist, present to us on the altar of sacrifice during Mass and on the altars of sacrifice of our daily living as we give ourselves over for the good of others. In this giving we learn who Jesus is.

◆ My manner of distributing Holy Communion reveals to communicants how I understand the eucharistic mystery in that . . .

Brief Silence

Prayer

As we encounter your divine Son, O God, in our daily lives and in our participation in the Holy Eucharist, may we become more like him in our own self-giving and one day come to share the fullness of Life with him. We ask this through Christ our Lord. **Amen.**

This gospel concludes our reading of John's Bread of Life discourse. Jesus invites us to stay with him or leave, to believe in him or not. Let us reflect on the choices we have made . . .

Prayer

What choice do we have, dear God, but to follow your divine Son's model and give ourselves over for the good of others? His gift of his Body and Blood is a pledge to us that we will never be alone in our daily self-giving, that he will always be there with his strengthening hand, that the demand for self-sacrifice is not so great as the gift he gives. May we respond faithfully to his Presence and gift. We ask this through Christ our Lord. **Amen.**

Gospel (John 6:60-69)

Many of Jesus' disciples who were listening said, "This saying is hard; who can accept it?" Since Jesus knew that his disciples were murmuring about this, he said to them, "Does this shock you? What if you were to see the Son of Man ascending to where he was before? It is the spirit that gives life, while the flesh is of no avail. The words I have spoken to you are Spirit and life. But there are some of you who do not believe." Jesus knew from the beginning the ones who would not believe and the one who would betray him. And he said, "For this reason I have told you that no one can come to me unless it is granted him by my Father."

As a result of this, many of his disciples returned to their former way of life and no longer accompanied him. Jesus then said to the Twelve, "Do you also want to leave?" Simon Peter answered him, "Master, to whom shall we go? You have the words of eternal life. We have come to believe and are convinced that you are the Holy One of God."

Brief Silence

For Reflection

The choice Jesus sets before the disciples in this gospel is deeper than simply "Do you also want to leave?" Jesus is inviting them to come to believe in who he is ("the Holy One of God" given as Bread from heaven) and what he offers (his own Body and Blood for eternal Life). Believing, however, is not mere verbal assent. It must become the lived conviction of choosing to stay with and in the risen Christ. Choosing to stay with Jesus is a way of living modeled on Jesus' own way of self-giving living.

Never before had God demanded so much of the people—to give one's life for others. To share in Jesus' Body and Blood demands of us this same kind of self-giving. Choosing to follow Jesus and accept his gift of Self to us is a challenge to see beyond the sacrifice of self-giving and continual dying for the sake of others to the Life that comes from this self-sacrifice. Self-giving always leads to new life and this is why we are able to make the choice to stay with the Master—he has "the words of eternal life."

✦ My eating and drinking the Body and Blood of Christ deepens my conviction about how I should live as a follower of the risen Christ in these ways . . .

Brief Silence

Prayer

Our Holy Communion strengthens us, O God, to follow Jesus faithfully, live his Gospel with integrity, and model his goodness and care for others. May his words of eternal Life touch us to empty ourselves of all that keeps us from growing in his love and compassion. May one day we enter into the fullness of Life with him. We ask this through Christ our Lord. **Amen.**

Jesus invites us to reflect on how and why we keep human and divine commandments. Let us ask God's mercy for the times we have not been faithful to the spirit of the law . . .

Prayer

God of the covenant, you give us commandments not to bind us, but to set us free. May we embrace your divine Law ever more faithfully, and through its guidance come to a deeper relationship with you, one built on the first commandment of all, that of love. We ask this through Christ our Lord. **Amen.**

Gospel (Mark 7:1-8, 14-15, 21-23)

When the Pharisees with some scribes who had come from Jerusalem gathered around Jesus, they observed that some of his disciples ate their meals with unclean, that is, unwashed, hands.—For the Pharisees and, in fact, all Jews, do not eat without carefully washing their hands, keeping the tradition of the elders. And on coming from the marketplace they do not eat without purifying themselves. And there are many other things that they have traditionally observed, the purification of cups and jugs and kettles and beds.—So the Pharisees and scribes questioned him, "Why do your disciples not follow the tradition of the elders but instead eat a meal with unclean hands?" He responded, "Well did Isaiah prophesy about you hypocrites, as it is written: / *This people honors me with their lips, / but their hearts are far from me; / in vain do they worship me, / teaching as doctrines human precepts.* / You disregard God's commandment but cling to human tradition."

He summoned the crowd again and said to them, "Hear me, all of you, and understand. Nothing that enters one from outside can defile that person; but the things that come out from within are what defile.

"From within people, from their hearts, come evil thoughts, unchastity, theft, murder, adultery, greed, malice, deceit, licentiousness, envy, blasphemy, arrogance, folly. All these evils come from within and they defile."

Brief Silence

For Reflection

In the gospel it appears that "the Pharisees with some scribes" are judging Jesus and his disciples for how they fail to keep the Jewish traditions. In fact, Jesus is passing judgment on the Pharisees and scribes by facing them with their own self-righteousness. The Pharisees fixate on keeping human traditions; Jesus frees people from rigid adherence to human traditions and redirects them to authentic living of God's commandments. At stake is right covenantal relationship with God and others in the community. Law is about right relationships, not about self-righteousness.

One can keep the letter of the law and miss entirely the point of the law—moral living is a sign of covenantal relationship with God. We who commit ourselves to following the risen Jesus don't merely keep the commandments; we know that the commandments are a sign of our faithful covenantal relationship with God. When our hearts are turned to God, we have life. This is what is at stake. God's Life is what unbinds us and gives us the ultimate freedom.

✦ My manner of distributing Holy Communion fosters deeper relationships with the risen Christ and with each other in that . . .

Brief Silence

Prayer

This sacrament of love, O God, forms us into your loving people whose hearts are turned toward you. May we be ever faithful to your many gifts to us and come to the ultimate freedom of living the Gospel as Jesus taught us. We ask this through Christ our Lord. **Amen.**

Jesus heals the deaf man with a speech impediment. As we prepare for our prayer and reflection, let us ask Jesus to open our ears to hear his word, touch our tongues to proclaim his praise, render our hearts to receive his mercy . . .

Prayer

Your words, O God, are life-giving salvation. As we grapple with the words you speak to us in so many ways, may we take them into our hearts and allow them to change us into being ever more perfect members of your divine Son's Body. We ask this through Christ our Lord. **Amen.**

Gospel (Mark 7:31-37)

Again Jesus left the district of Tyre and went by way of Sidon to the Sea of Galilee, into the district of the Decapolis. And people brought to him a deaf man who had a speech impediment and begged him to lay his hand on him. He took him off by himself away from the crowd. He put his finger into the man's ears and, spitting, touched his tongue; then he looked up to heaven and groaned, and said to him, *"Ephphatha!"*—that is, "Be opened!"— And immediately the man's ears were opened, his speech impediment was removed, and he spoke plainly. He ordered them not to tell anyone. But the more he ordered them not to, the more they proclaimed it. They were exceedingly astonished and they said, "He has done all things well. He makes the deaf hear and the mute speak."

Brief Silence

For Reflection

In this gospel Jesus opens the ears and loosens the tongue of the deaf-mute. Both he and the crowd cannot contain themselves, but proclaim what Jesus has done. What has Jesus really done? Healed the man? Yes, but more. Jesus has revealed that he is far more than a miracle worker, as fascinating and wonderful as that may be. Understood only as an external sign, however, the miracle falls short of the reality. The miracles Jesus performs reveal his own divine power, his own compassion for the human condition, his own mission. What must be proclaimed is not the sign itself, but that to which it points: God's Presence bringing salvation. Faced with this revelation, no one can keep silent. The Word grants the power of word.

We surmise that something very profound must have happened between Jesus and the deaf man even before the miracle that brought the deaf and mute man to an intensified insight about Jesus. Jesus must have communicated something to him that resonated deep within the man's very being and changed him. This is why he could not help but proclaim the miracle—his encounter with Jesus changed him.

✦ When I say the words "Body of Christ" or "Blood of Christ," I am proclaiming . . .

Brief Silence

Prayer

You are present to us, dear God, in the many people and events of our daily living. As we encounter you, help us to have the courage to proclaim your goodness to us, your compassion and care, your great love for each of us. Bring us to the fullness of Life your word makes known. We ask this through Christ our Lord. **Amen.**

Jesus makes known that he is "the Christ" who will suffer, die, and rise. Let us prepare ourselves to hear his words and his call to follow him through death to new Life . . .

Prayer

So often, O God, we misunderstand your will for us. Like Peter in the gospel, we have our own understanding of who Jesus is and what following him means. Open our ears and hearts to a new and deeper understanding of who Jesus is and the real demands of following him. Give us strength and perseverance. We ask this through Christ our Lord. **Amen.**

Gospel (Mark 8:27-35)

Jesus and his disciples set out for the villages of Caesarea Philippi. Along the way he asked his disciples, "Who do people say that I am?" They said in reply, "John the Baptist, others Elijah, still others one of the prophets." And he asked them, "But who do you say that I am?" Peter said to him in reply, "You are the Christ." Then he warned them not to tell anyone about him.

He began to teach them that the Son of Man must suffer greatly and be rejected by the elders, the chief priests, and the scribes, and be killed, and rise after three days. He spoke this openly. Then Peter took him aside and began to rebuke him. At this he turned around and, looking at his disciples, rebuked Peter and said, "Get behind me, Satan. You are thinking not as God does, but as human beings do."

He summoned the crowd with his disciples and said to them, "Whoever wishes to come after me must deny himself, take up his cross, and follow me. For whoever wishes to save his life will lose it, but whoever loses his life for my sake and that of the gospel will save it."

Brief Silence

For Reflection

The disciples are hardly prepared for understanding Jesus' identity as "the Christ"; they are even less prepared to grasp the demands of following him. Jesus is called "the Christ"—Peter is called Satan. Salvation confronts human resistance. Peter had a certain image, belief, expectation of what "the Christ" was to be, to do. Suffering, rejection, and being killed had nothing to do with Peter's Christ. But they have everything to do with the Christ of God. Without a right understanding of "the Christ," we cannot, with him, rise to new Life. Alone, the demands of discipleship would be impossible, the struggle beyond us. But with God as our help, we can begin to think as God does, not as humans. And how does God think? Not in terms of beatings, buffets, pain, ridicule, or even death. God thinks in terms of life and love. God thinks in terms of salvation. God only wills for us what is good for us and what brings us to new Life. We take up our own cross daily because this is the way to a share in risen Life.

✦ My ministry has everything to do with "the Christ" of God in that . . .

Brief Silence

Prayer

Loving God, your Son's gift of himself in the Eucharist is strength for our journey of daily dying to self so that we might rise to new Life in him. The cross we bear is so small in relation to the gift you give us. May our hearts be ever grateful for being called to live as Jesus did and to one day come to share in his everlasting glory. We ask this through Christ our Lord. **Amen.**

Jesus teaches the disciples in this gospel about who they ought to be: servants of all. Let us ask God's mercy for the times we have put ourselves before others . . .

Prayer

Your call to us, gracious God, is to overcome our tendency to seek our own glory and become the least so we can serve others. Strengthen us for this way of living, one modeled so well by Jesus. May we come to a deeper understanding that serving others is our greatest dignity. We ask this through Christ our Lord. **Amen.**

Gospel (Mark 9:30-37)

Jesus and his disciples left from there and began a journey through Galilee, but he did not wish anyone to know about it. He was teaching his disciples and telling them, "The Son of Man is to be handed over to men and they will kill him, and three days after his death the Son of Man will rise." But they did not understand the saying, and they were afraid to question him.

They came to Capernaum and, once inside the house, he began to ask them, "What were you arguing about on the way?" But they remained silent. They had been discussing among themselves on the way who was the greatest. Then he sat down, called the Twelve, and said to them, "If anyone wishes to be first, he shall be the last of all and the servant of all." Taking a child, he placed it in their midst, and putting his arms around it, he said to them, "Whoever receives one child such as this in my name, receives me; and whoever receives me, receives not me but the One who sent me."

Brief Silence

For Reflection

Children are innocent and without pretensions. They naturally embody what "least of all" means. This also illustrates to what extent the disciple is to become the "servant of all" by receiving even the "least of all." The total self-emptying that enables one to receive the "least of all" describes the disciple. This is how we receive Jesus—by receiving the least. No one is insignificant. Everyone is worth dying for.

The scandal of this gospel is that Jesus, the leader and teacher of the disciples, will be reduced to the least when he is handed over and dies. How do the disciples react to this scandalous teaching? They argue among themselves about who is the greatest! Jesus rightly reduces them to silence. The disciples do not understand greatest and least, first and last, servant of all. They do not understand that Jesus' own death is a call to die to self, to choose to become the greatest by being the least. Confronted with this saving mystery, we ought to all be reduced to silence—but now for the right reason.

✦ Distributing the Body (Blood) of Christ requires my dying to self in that . . .

Brief Silence

Prayer

Gracious God, in the gift of the Holy Eucharist we are nourished to serve others, to accept becoming the least. In this heavenly Food you bring us to the greatness of a share in your divine Life. May we always and everywhere be faithful and grateful. We ask this through Christ our Lord. **Amen.**

Discipleship calls us to make radical choices about how we live as followers of Jesus. We ask God's pardon for the times we have failed and for the strength to be faithful disciples . . .

Prayer

Merciful God, you see our human weakness and sinfulness, yet you are ever faithful to us in offering us your Life and salvation. May we have the courage to cut off whatever keeps us from growing in our love for you and others. May our sinfulness decrease and our goodness increase. We ask this through Christ our Lord. **Amen.**

Gospel (Mark 9:38-43, 45, 47-48)

At that time, John said to Jesus, "Teacher, we saw someone driving out demons in your name, and we tried to prevent him because he does not follow us." Jesus replied, "Do not prevent him. There is no one who performs a mighty deed in my name who can at the same time speak ill of me. For whoever is not against us is for us. Anyone who gives you a cup of water to drink because you belong to Christ, amen, I say to you, will surely not lose his reward.

"Whoever causes one of these little ones who believe in me to sin, it would be better for him if a great millstone were put around his neck and he were thrown into the sea. If your hand causes you to sin, cut it off. It is better for you to enter into life maimed than with two hands to go into Gehenna, into the unquenchable fire. And if your foot causes you to sin, cut if off. It is better for you to enter into life crippled than with two feet to be thrown into Gehenna. And if your eye causes you to sin, pluck it out. Better for you to enter into the kingdom of God with one eye than with two eyes to be thrown into Gehenna, where 'their worm does not die, and the fire is not quenched.'"

Brief Silence

For Reflection

Focused completely on his saving mission to bring about the kingdom of God, Jesus directly confronts human pettiness and sinfulness. He uses graphic examples to demand that disciples turn from whatever is inconsistent with acting in his name, with continuing his mission. Any behavior which causes us to sin or to lead others into sin must be cut off. Part of a disciple's work is to take on Jesus' values, Jesus' goodness. Being a disciple demands radical choices about how we live and relate to others.

Discipleship is decided by our *behavior* rather than by our being identified with a particular group or not. What is crucial to discipleship is how we act. Jesus uses extreme terms to tell us that we must turn from whatever is inconsistent with acting in his name. Any behavior which causes us to sin or to lead others into sin must be cut off. We are to root out the cause of sin in us at all costs—root out whatever is not consistent with our attraction to who Jesus is. What is at stake is "enter[ing] into the kingdom of God," entering into fullness of Life.

✦ When I am completely focused on my ministry and what it means, I . . .

Brief Silence

Prayer

Your kingdom, O God, is one of truth and Life, goodness and mercy. Nourish us with the gift of your Son's Body and Blood so that we might be more faithful in living as Jesus taught us and one day enter into the fullness of Life with you. We ask this through Christ our Lord. **Amen.**

The Pharisees in this gospel show hardness of heart when they test Jesus. Let us begin our prayer and reflection by examining our own heart and ask for the healing embrace of Jesus . . .

Prayer

We confess, O God, that sometimes we are hard of heart. Turn our hearts toward you, so that we might turn ourselves toward others in love and care. May we embrace others as Jesus embraces us. We ask this through Christ our Lord. **Amen.**

Gospel (Mark 10:2-16)

The Pharisees approached Jesus and asked, "Is it lawful for a husband to divorce his wife?" They were testing him. He said to them in reply, "What did Moses command you?" They replied, "Moses permitted a husband to write a bill of divorce and dismiss her." But Jesus told them, "Because of the hardness of your hearts he wrote you this commandment. But from the beginning of creation, *God made them male and female. For this reason a man shall leave his father and mother and be joined to his wife, and the two shall become one flesh.* So they are no longer two but one flesh. Therefore what God has joined together, no human being must separate." In the house the disciples again questioned Jesus about this. He said to them, "Whoever divorces his wife and marries another commits adultery against her; and if she divorces her husband and marries another, she commits adultery."

And people were bringing children to him that he might touch them, but the disciples rebuked them. When Jesus saw this he became indignant and said to them, "Let the children come to me; do not prevent them, for the kingdom of God belongs to such as these. Amen, I say to you, whoever does not accept the kingdom of God like a child will not enter it." Then he embraced them and blessed them, placing his hands on them.

Brief Silence

For Reflection

The longer form of this Sunday's gospel unfolds in two interrelated situations. The Pharisees approach Jesus to test him about his stance concerning marriage and divorce; the disciples rebuke the people for bringing their children to Jesus. In both situations, God's intentions for human relationships are being thwarted. In both situations, Jesus upholds human relationships as fundamental to embracing the kingdom of God. In both situations, faithful ones are embraced and blessed by God. In this gospel Jesus exposes the hardness of the Pharisees' hearts. This challenges us to look deep within our own hearts.

In the deepest recesses of our hearts, we all desire to live in union with one another as God intends. The gospel intimates that the kingdom of God belongs to those who yield "hardness of . . . hearts" to the open embrace Jesus models. Just as the gospel moves from shortsighted confrontation over Mosaic laws of divorce to Jesus' tender embrace of little children, so must our lives move from our own shortsightedness to the wide embrace of God's ultimate plan—hearts turned toward God and each other in relationships that are holy.

✦ I am hard of heart when . . . What softens my heart is . . .

Brief Silence

Prayer

O good God, Holy Communion is a divine embrace of union with you that makes us holy in your sight. May our holiness spill over into compassion and care for others, that we might serve you faithfully all our days and one day enjoy fullness of union with you in everlasting Life. We ask this through Christ our Lord. **Amen.**

The man in the gospel kept all God's commandments, but he was not able to do the one thing more Jesus asked of him. Let us ask God's mercy for the times we have not done what Jesus asks of us . . .

Prayer

Our possessiveness of the things we have, O God, is a sign of our divided hearts. May your glance of love melt our hearts so that we turn toward you, resolved to follow more single-heartedly Jesus' Gospel way of living. We ask this through Christ our Lord. **Amen.**

Gospel (Mark 10:17-27)

As Jesus was setting out on a journey, a man ran up, knelt down before him, and asked him, "Good teacher, what must I do to inherit eternal life?" Jesus answered him, "Why do you call me good? No one is good but God alone. You know the commandments: *You shall not kill; you shall not commit adultery; you shall not steal; you shall not bear false witness; you shall not defraud; honor your father and your mother.*" He replied and said to him, "Teacher, all of these I have observed from my youth." Jesus, looking at him, loved him and said to him, "You are lacking in one thing. Go, sell what you have, and give to the poor and you will have treasure in heaven; then come, follow me." At that statement his face fell, and he went away sad, for he had many possessions.

Jesus looked around and said to his disciples, "How hard it is for those who have wealth to enter the kingdom of God!" The disciples were amazed at his words. So Jesus again said to them in reply, "Children, how hard it is to enter the kingdom of God! It is easier for a camel to pass through the eye of a needle than for one who is rich to enter the kingdom of God." They were exceedingly astonished and said among themselves, "Then who can be saved?" Jesus looked at them and said, "For human beings it is impossible, but not for God. All things are possible for God."

Brief Silence

For Reflection

The man must have had an inkling that keeping the commandments was not enough, or else he never would have approached Jesus with his question about how to inherit eternal Life. In spite of his faithfulness in keeping God's commandments and his being loved by Jesus, the man nevertheless had a divided heart: "he went away sad, for he had many possessions." The man needed to turn his focus from earthly life to eternal Life, from possessions (and, yes, even God's commandments) to single-heartedly following Jesus to salvation. Where is our heart? Are we overjoyed at Jesus' glance of love, or are we sad because it is too much?

Giving our all to follow Jesus doesn't mean that we literally sell everything; we all have family and social obligations that make having things a necessity. Jesus is saying that we can't let possessions (or anything else, for that matter) divide our hearts. Too often possessions possess us; we must let go so only God possesses us. Riches are a stumbling block to following Jesus when they command our attention so that we are not turned toward doing right—which is what following Jesus means.

✦ As Jesus looked upon the man in the gospel with love, I look upon each communicant with love when I . . . and they . . .

Brief Silence

Prayer

Holy Communion is such a wondrous glance of love, gracious God! You nourish us with the Bread of Life and the divine love that leads us to salvation. May our hearts never be divided in the face of this great mystery, but always turned toward you with our own love and gratitude. We ask this through Christ our Lord. **Amen.**

Jesus teaches us that our glory lies in serving others. Let us prepare for our prayer and reflection by asking the Lord Jesus to forgive us for the times we have sought glory for ourselves in other ways . . .

Prayer

Oh, how attractive to us is honor and glory! We beg you, O God, to empty our hearts of our vain seeking of the wrong things and strengthen us to embrace the life of servanthood Jesus taught us. We ask this through Christ our Lord. **Amen.**

Gospel (Mark 10:35-45)

James and John, the sons of Zebedee, came to Jesus and said to him, "Teacher, we want you to do for us whatever we ask of you." He replied, "What do you wish me to do for you?" They answered him, "Grant that in your glory we may sit one at your right and the other at your left." Jesus said to them, "You do not know what you are asking. Can you drink the cup that I drink or be baptized with the baptism with which I am baptized?" They said to him, "We can." Jesus said to them, "The cup that I drink, you will drink, and with the baptism with which I am baptized, you will be baptized; but to sit at my right or at my left is not mine to give but is for those for whom it has been prepared." When the ten heard this, they became indignant at James and John. Jesus summoned them and said to them, "You know that those who are recognized as rulers over the Gentiles lord it over them, and their great ones make their authority over them felt. But it shall not be so among you. Rather, whoever wishes to be great among you will be your servant; whoever wishes to be first among you will be the slave of all. For the Son of Man did not come to be served but to serve and to give his life as a ransom for many."

Brief Silence

For Reflection

Why did the apostles follow Jesus? This gospel suggests they had reward on their minds: the glory of sitting at the right and left of Jesus in positions of honor. It took the apostles a long time to learn that the real reward of following Jesus would be to "drink the cup" and "be baptized" with his baptism. His baptism was his lifelong choice to do the will of the Father no matter what the cost. The cost would be humbly serving others to the point even of giving his life "for many." As Jesus' followers, we can choose no less. Like the apostles, it takes us no less time to learn this.

Jesus responds to the apostles' request for a share in his glory by saying that discipleship isn't about raw power ("lord it over them," "make their authority felt"). Discipleship is about servanthood, even when it entails suffering and giving one's life. The only way to glory is by self-emptying, serving, giving one's life. The apostles weren't ready for this—they abandoned Jesus at his passion and death. Are we ready to follow? Are we ready to choose our baptism into his suffering and death?

✦ The "cup that I drink" and offer to others during my ministry demands that I live in service of others in that . . .

Brief Silence

Prayer

The road to glory, gracious God, is by embracing the transformation of self that Eucharist makes available to us. Through the Life you give us, may we more faithfully give over our life for the good of others. We ask this through Christ our Lord. **Amen.**

Bartimaeus the blind beggar cries out in faith to Jesus. Let us ask for God's mercy for the times we have lacked the faith to cry out to Jesus . . .

Prayer

Compassionate and healing God, you constantly act on our behalf, ever so surely and gently leading us to salvation. May we have the faith and conviction of Bartimaeus, act without reserve in living the Gospel, and deepen our faith as we grow in our relationship with you and each other. We ask this through Christ our Lord. **Amen.**

Gospel (Mark 10:46-52)

As Jesus was leaving Jericho with his disciples and a sizable crowd, Bartimaeus, a blind man, the son of Timaeus, sat by the roadside begging. On hearing that it was Jesus of Nazareth, he began to cry out and say, "Jesus, son of David, have pity on me." And many rebuked him, telling him to be silent. But he kept calling out all the more, "Son of David, have pity on me." Jesus stopped and said, "Call him." So they called the blind man, saying to him, "Take courage; get up, Jesus is calling you." He threw aside his cloak, sprang up, and came to Jesus. Jesus said to him in reply, "What do you want me to do for you?" The blind man replied to him, "Master, I want to see." Jesus told him, "Go your way; your faith has saved you." Immediately he received his sight and followed him on the way.

Brief Silence

For Reflection

The verbs describing Bartimaeus's actions in this gospel say everything about faith, encountering Jesus, and choosing to follow him. He cried out, kept calling, threw aside his cloak, sprang up and came to Jesus, stated his request, received his sight, followed Jesus. Such need, such urgency, such conviction, such action, such faith! These verbs describe Bartimaeus's faith-in-action, his deepening relationship with Jesus. Faith is the insight and cause of action. So must it be for us.

Without persistence in prayer and seeking encounters with Jesus, it will be impossible for us to follow him faithfully. Encounters with Jesus in prayer keep our relationship to him growing, keep our relationship with him healthy and strong. The Gospel way of living, the rhythm of dying and rising, plays itself out in many ways—this Sunday in a rhythm of faith and action. In practical, everyday terms this means that at times we are *doing* our faith—reaching out to those around us in need. At other times we are *being* our faith—taking time to savor our relationship with God.

✦ My distributing Holy Communion is my faith-in-action when I . . .

Brief Silence

Prayer

Participating faithfully in the eucharistic action, O ever-living and loving God, is our way of expressing our great desire to deepen our relationship with you. May this holy sacrament bring us to everlasting Life with you. We ask this through Christ our Lord. **Amen.**

**As we honor the saints who have
been faithful to Gospel living during
our prayer and reflection, let us ask
for God's mercy for the times we
have been unfaithful . . .**

Prayer

Blessed are you, God of holiness! May
we embrace your compassion and care,
forgiveness and mercy, love and self-giving and thus model your
divine Presence among us. Increase our holiness, so that our lives
might be more worthy of the gift of your divine Presence that
dwells among and within us. We ask this through Christ our Lord.
Amen.

Gospel (Matt 5:1-12a)

When Jesus saw the crowds, he went up the mountain, and after
he had sat down, his disciples came to him. He began to teach
them, saying: / "Blessed are the poor in spirit, / for theirs is the
Kingdom of heaven. / Blessed are they who mourn, / for they will
be comforted. / Blessed are the meek, / for they will inherit the
land. / Blessed are they who hunger and thirst for righteousness, /
for they will be satisfied. / Blessed are the merciful, / for they will
be shown mercy. / Blessed are the clean of heart, / for they will see
God. / Blessed are the peacemakers, / for they will be called children of God. / Blessed are they who are persecuted for the sake of
righteousness, / for theirs is the Kingdom of heaven. / Blessed are
you when they insult you and persecute you and utter every kind
of evil against you falsely because of me. Rejoice and be glad, for
your reward will be great in heaven."

Brief Silence

For Reflection

It is no accident that the Gospel of Matthew has Jesus go "up the mountain," traditionally a place associated with divine encounter, to teach the Beatitudes to his disciples. The Beatitudes reveal the very Being of God ("Blessed," holy), God's care for God's beloved people ("poor in spirit," "those who mourn," etc.), God's intent for faithful ones ("theirs is the kingdom of heaven"). The Beatitudes reveal the mind and heart of God. Those who have encountered God and lived the Beatitudes have the same mind and heart. We call them "saints." There is a countless multitude of saints in heaven endlessly singing God's praises. There is a countless multitude of saints here among us who have embraced the beatific, Godlike way of living. While this feast day primarily honors the saints who have gone before us, we cannot forget ourselves on this day. This solemnity reminds us that our life of blessedness rests on an intimate relationship with God and each other expressed through enduring bonds of mutual care, mercy, humility, and self-giving.

✦ I encounter God and learn the divine mind and heart when . . .

Brief Silence

Prayer

Through our participation in the Holy Eucharist, gift-giving God, you bring us to greater Life and holiness. Help us to live in a way faithful to your gifts, and one day share with you everlasting Life. We ask this through Christ our Lord. **Amen.**

We commemorate the faithfulness of the souls in purgatory and pray that they might soon come to the fullness of risen Life. We pause to open ourselves to the great mystery of God's mercy . . .

Prayer

We pray this day, O God, for our beloved departed, that they come to the fullness of eternal Life you offer to all of us. May they be for us an inspiration of victory, that as we pray for them we also join them in offering you honor and glory. We ask this through Christ our Lord. **Amen.**

Gospel (John 6:37-40)

Jesus said to the crowds: "Everything that the Father gives me will come to me, and I will not reject anyone who comes to me, because I came down from heaven not to do my own will but the will of the one who sent me. And this is the will of the one who sent me, that I should not lose anything of what he gave me, but that I should raise it on the last day. For this is the will of my Father, that everyone who sees the Son and believes in him may have eternal life, and I shall raise him on the last day."

Brief Silence

For Reflection

We generally think of God's will as meaning what God wants *us* to do—obey God's laws. In this gospel God's will means what *God* wants to do—raise us up to have eternal Life. This day we celebrate the hope we have for our faithful departed, because of God's gracious will for each of us. The amazing assurance of this gospel is a clear statement of what God *wills* for us: God *wills* that we all be saved ("this is the will of my father . . . everyone . . . may have eternal life") and this has already been accomplished in Christ. God our Father extends divine generosity and love toward us in Christ for the wildest wish possible: that we "have eternal life" and are raised up with Christ "on the last day."

The souls in purgatory are like all of us weak human creatures; they have sinned. But they also have already won the victory. All that remains is the satisfaction for their weak moments and righting their relationships with God and others in the Body of Christ. We pray for them as brothers and sisters in Christ, in the communion of saints.

✦ What God wants me to do is . . . What God wants to do for me is . . .

Brief Silence

Prayer

Saying yes to your divine will, O God, assures us of one day joining all the saints in heaven to offer you eternal praise and thanksgiving. As we receive Holy Communion, the pledge of eternal Life, may we grow in our willingness to serve you and always accomplish your divine will for us. We ask this through Christ our Lord. **Amen.**

Other gospel options for November 2:

Matthew 5:1-12a / Matthew 11:25-30 / Matthew 25:31-46 / Luke 7:11-17 / Luke 23:44-46, 50, 52-53; 24:1-6a / Luke 24:13-16, 28-35 / John 5:24-29 / John 6:51-58 / John 11:17-27 / John 11:32-45 / John 14:1-6

The gospel tells about the poor widow who gave two small coins to the temple treasury. Let us look into our hearts and see what we are prepared to give to the Lord Jesus during our prayer and reflection . . .

Prayer

Living and loving God, you gave your Son to us as a model for giving our all for others. May we take to heart his Gospel and reach out to others with all our own being, thus serving you in one another. We ask this through Christ our Lord. **Amen.**

Gospel (Mark 12:38-44)

In the course of his teaching Jesus said to the crowds, "Beware of the scribes, who like to go around in long robes and accept greetings in the marketplaces, seats of honor in synagogues, and places of honor at banquets. They devour the houses of widows and, as a pretext recite lengthy prayers. They will receive a very severe condemnation."

He sat down opposite the treasury and observed how the crowd put money into the treasury. Many rich people put in large sums. A poor widow also came and put in two small coins worth a few cents. Calling his disciples to himself, he said to them, "Amen, I say to you, this poor widow put in more than all the other contributors to the treasury. For they have all contributed from their surplus wealth, but she, from her poverty, has contributed all she had, her whole livelihood."

Brief Silence

For Reflection

Jesus teaches the crowds to beware of the hypocrisy of the scribes who know God's word and law, yet seek places of honor and hurt those whom the law demands they protect—the widows. Jesus condemns them severely. "Calling his disciples to himself," he teaches them that they are not to do like the scribes. They are instead to do like the widow in the temple who gives all she has. True disciples give all they have, their whole livelihood—not goods, but *themselves*. The *amount* of what we have and give is really not important at all in the long run. What is important is how we regard and care for others; how we fulfill our responsibilities in the community; how we embrace the unlimited possibilities of deeper relationships, new riches, everlasting Life.

Disciples are to give all they have without counting the cost, calculating self-gain, or seeking attention. The amazing thing about faithful discipleship is that God provides us with astonishing surplus: protection, talents, blessings. The "whole livelihood" disciples give is their very selves; disciples give of what God has already given them. Ultimately, discipleship is about good stewardship of who we are.

✦ At every eucharistic celebration, Jesus gives fully of himself to us, and so my response is to give . . .

Brief Silence

Prayer

We will never want, gracious God, for you feed us abundantly with the Bread of Life and Cup of Salvation. May our response be as self-giving as the widow's, and as loving as your divine Son. We ask this through Christ our Lord. **Amen.**

This gospel speaks of the tribulations accompanying Jesus' Second Coming; it also assures us of his nearness now. Let us ask God's mercy for the times we have not been attentive to Jesus' nearness . . .

Prayer

O God, in you time is an everlasting now. Help us not to worry about the future because we have lived good lives in the now. May we never take our eyes from you, who teaches us all goodness and just living. We ask this through Christ our Lord. **Amen.**

Gospel (Mark 13:24-32)

Jesus said to his disciples: "In those days after that tribulation the sun will be darkened, and the moon will not give its light, and the stars will be falling from the sky, and the powers in the heavens will be shaken.

"And then they will see 'the Son of Man coming in the clouds' with great power and glory, and then he will send out the angels and gather his elect from the four winds, from the end of the earth to the end of the sky.

"Learn a lesson from the fig tree. When its branch becomes tender and sprouts leaves, you know that summer is near. In the same way, when you see these things happening, know that he is near, at the gates. Amen, I say to you, this generation will not pass away until all these things have taken place. Heaven and earth will pass away, but my words will not pass away.

"But of that day or hour, no one knows, neither the angels in heaven, nor the Son, but only the Father."

Brief Silence

For Reflection

Jesus predicted several times the coming end of his earthly life, which was not too far into the future. The disciples could not hear what Jesus was teaching; they could not envision a future such as Jesus predicted. In this gospel, too, he teaches about the future; however, this time his words deal with an unknown, distant future, with cosmic events, with his final coming in power to overcome darkness, and with his drawing the elect into the light of his final glory. Jesus uses the image of the greening of "the fig tree" when summer is near as a sign that "he is near." Summer is a time of life, growth, fruitfulness. Those who hear and heed his words are in the greening of their lives; they choose for themselves life, growth, fruitfulness.

There is a wonderful play in this gospel between a future event that we cannot even imagine and the "now" in which we are immersed and is very real to us. Because Jesus "is near," the future and present are not separated by a distance of time, but are united by the nearness of Person.

✦ My manner of distributing Holy Communion indicates that the future coming of Jesus is now when I . . .

Brief Silence

Prayer

Holy Communion brings us Life, O God, and we are grateful for this wondrous gift. May we grow ever closer to the risen Jesus as we seek to live the Life he gained for us, and one day come to share in his eternal glory. We ask this through Christ our Lord. **Amen.**

We acclaim Christ as our King. Let us look into our hearts and see how Christ is enthroned there . . .

Prayer

O God, as we honor your divine Son as our King and Savior, we ask you to increase in us our commitment to love with our very lives as he has loved us. May we seek his kingdom, which is to do your holy will. We ask this through Christ our Lord. **Amen.**

Gospel (John 18:33b-37)

Pilate said to Jesus, "Are you the King of the Jews?" Jesus answered, "Do you say this on your own or have others told you about me?" Pilate answered, "I am not a Jew, am I? Your own nation and the chief priests handed you over to me. What have you done?" Jesus answered, "My kingdom does not belong to this world. If my kingdom did belong to this world, my attendants would be fighting to keep me from being handed over to the Jews. But as it is, my kingdom is not here." So Pilate said to him, "Then you are a king?" Jesus answered, "You say I am a king. For this I was born and for this I came into the world, to testify to the truth. Everyone who belongs to the truth listens to my voice."

Brief Silence

For Reflection

In this gospel conversation Pilate questions Jesus about his identity ("Are you the King of the Jews?") and about why he is on trial ("What have you done?"). What unfolds is a conversation about two very different worlds. That of Pilate and the chief priests, in which fighting, falsehood, and obstinacy predominate. That of Jesus, in which life, truth, and openness prevail. Yes, Jesus is a King—but of a kingdom different from Herod's. What he has done is reveal a kingdom that "does not belong to this world," but is meant to transform it. From evil to goodness. From sinfulness to salvation. From death to life.

We clearly see that Jesus' kingdom is not of this world. Christ's kingdom is not a spatial place ("does not belong to this world"), but an interior identity defined by our relationship to Christ the King. This Sunday we celebrate a King whose Presence and power we have already experienced: Christ, whose kingdom is not territory but virtue, not power but service, not wealth but grace. This King has loved us with his very life.

✦ I live in Pilate's world when I . . . I live in Jesus' kingdom when I . . .

Brief Silence

Prayer

Good and gracious God, the gifts you give us are beyond compare. Your divine Son continues to show us his love by giving us his very Body and Blood for our nourishment. May it strengthen us to serve him in others faithfully, and one day share in the everlasting kingdom of his glory. We ask this through Christ our Lord. **Amen.**